MAN...
CHURC... ...OKSTALL

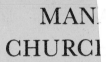

MANAGING THE CHURCH BOOKSTALL

Prepared by

The Religious Book Foundation

HODDER AND STOUGHTON
LONDON SYDNEY AUCKLAND TORONTO

British Library Cataloguing in Publication Data

Religious Book Foundation
    Managing the church bookstall.
    1. Christian literature – Publication and distribution
    I. Title
    658.89'0705'73   Z286.R4

    ISBN 0 340 25893 4

CONTENTS

INTRODUCTION

These pages include the thoughts of a large number of people who have given their advice, in many cases based upon long experience in dealing with books; in particular, among booksellers and bookstall people whose comments are reflected here, special recognition is given to Georgette Butcher of Scripture Union and Frank Hill of Mowbrays. They, among others, will recognise Aphorisms, Blunders, Catches, Dicta . . . in this compact introduction to Bookstall Management, which is more than an ABC, because even the experienced bookstall person is likely to find some useful hints on making a better job of it.

Chapters 8 and 9 are contributed by Jennifer Franklin and Beryl Goodland respectively. They offer practical experience of what happens when the ideas conveyed in the earlier chapters are put into action—and when they are not! These two chapters, as well as the rest of the book, offer an insight into approaches which have proved effective—useful both to the tyro and to the expert.

The major part of preparing the book has been carried out by Myrtle Powley who has succeeded in presenting the basics in readable style and sprinkled with do's and don'ts. Summaries at the end of each chapter are check lists for future action. The Appendixes offer suggestions for reference or background reading; meanwhile, here is sufficient information to put the bookstall and its management into clear focus.

This publication was a cherished project of the Religious Book Foundation, especially of its first Secretary, Guy Hitchings, who tenaciously clung to the idea that it should be written. Our thanks to Edward England of Hodder and Stoughton for undertaking its publication.

Lastly, our grateful thanks to all who have readily granted permission for quotations which are acknowledged in the following pages, especially to the Archdeacon of Norwich, The Ven. Tim Dudley-Smith, for extracts from *Christian Literature and the Church Bookstall*. The enthusiasm which he and many others have exhibited on behalf of books in the service of the Christian Church, and the whole community, is contagious— may all who read this book catch that enthusiasm.

Peter J. Lardi, on behalf of
The Religious Book Foundation

I

Why a Church Bookstall?

At the heart of the Christian faith there is the word: Christ the eternal Word of God, incarnate in our human flesh, living our life and speaking our language; and the word of God spoken through the prophets, evangelists and apostles, committed to parchment and papyrus—and in time translated, printed and bound between covers, to be sold over the counter of your local bookshop.

Every Christian who can read, needs a Bible. Wherever Christians have taken their faith, they have taught the people to read and given them the Scriptures in their own language. We, who speak and read English, have the advantage of numerous translations and versions of the Bible from which to choose. Probably just about every literate English-speaking Christian owns a Bible, or a part of one.

Owning a Bible is just the beginning.

'Do you understand what you are reading?' asked Philip the evangelist of the Ethiopian Chancellor, who had just bought his first copy of the Scriptures.

9

'How can I understand unless someone explains it to me?' the man replied.

Had such things existed then, Philip would no doubt, as well as expounding the word to his new convert, have sent him on his way with a set of Bible-reading notes, a practical booklet on How to Continue in the Christian Life, and a recommendation to buy a commentary on the Book of Isaiah when he got home. As it was, the man had only the memory of a life-giving conversation—and his scroll of Isaiah. Yet even out of that small beginning, tradition says, grew the church of Christ in Ethiopia.

Why is it that we today, who have so much good Christian literature at our disposal, are often content to rely for our teaching largely on the spoken word? Try to remember in detail a sermon which, at the time you heard it, really inspired you—or a religious radio broadcast, or television programme. The spoken word has a habit of slipping from the mind, however powerful its impact at the time.

Timothy Dudley-Smith, himself both preacher and writer, emphasised this point in his book *Christian Literature and the Church Bookstall*, published in 1963.

> Let the clergyman be never so convincing on Easter Sunday over the evidences for the resurrection, by the time Trinity comes round few of his hearers will hold their own in a discussion with an informed rationalist. But let them have at home, in their own possession, a booklet on the subject to refresh their memories, and to

guide their studies of the gospel records, and it will be a different story . . . Printed publications can go with us even when we are alone; they are always ready to speak to us, in our beds at night, in the open air, when travelling, at our own fireside. If there is light to see by, no minute of the day falls outside their working hours. And when, through circumstances of time or distance, regard for privacy, or respect for grief, other voices fall silent, these silent voices will continue.

A book is always there on the shelf to be constantly referred to, re-read, or lent to others. To have this ministry of the word in permanent form is a priceless asset for which many Christians in less fortunate countries may well envy us.

'Through books,' someone has said, 'we have access to the greatest minds and the greatest literature, not only of our own time, but of all time.' Christian books can bring us the accumulated wisdom of the world's greatest Christians.

So why don't we make more use of them?

One answer is that many churchgoers have simply no idea of the enormous variety of Christian books available.

This is where the church bookstall comes in. Through a well-run bookstall, churchgoers who may never have entered a Christian bookshop (perhaps for the very good reason that there is none in their area), who have no idea of the richness of the reading matter available, who maybe are not used to reading very much at all, can be encouraged, in the words of Timothy Dudley-Smith, 'to learn how to live fruitful Christian lives; to learn how to serve Christ; to learn how to speak and witness for Him; to learn how to study the Bible and its doctrines; to learn how to expound the Scriptures; to learn how to teach in a Sunday school; to learn how to tackle the problems of Christian conduct.'

Every church ought to consider the advantages of having a bookstall. The fact that you are reading this book at all indicates that you are interested in the possibility of organising one. This may be because you are concerned that Christians should learn more about their faith, or because you are a book addict and want to share your enthusiasm with others. The first reason alone is a good enough motive; but a touch of the second will go a long way towards making it a success. What you need most of all, though, is practical know-how, and that is what this book hopes to offer.

Who reads books?

According to recent surveys we spend about half of our thirty-eight hours of leisure time each week watching TV, and only two hours a week reading books. And those are only *average* figures. About a third of the population never opens a book at all . . . The Book Promotion Feasibility Study indicated that no less than '48 per cent of the adult population either never visit a bookshop, or visit a bookshop less frequently than once a month'.

So wrote the Creative Director of Book Club Associates in 1977 (in *Selling the Book*, edited by Sydney Hyde).

The Book Marketing Council's report in April 1979 presents a slightly more optimistic picture.

> In general it is probably true to say that about a third of the adult population do not read books at all, and getting on for half are non-readers, or very light readers. Women read more than men, the young tend to read more than the old and the higher social classes read more than the lower social classes.

However, the report points out that these figures probably represent books *read* rather than books *used* (such as reference books, practical handbooks, cookery books, etc.).

Figures published regularly in *The Bookseller* indicate that the number of religious books published each quarter falls somewhere between fifth and seventh in the order of the various categories listed, below Fiction, Children's books, Politics and Economics, and History and Biography. Every year, about twelve hundred new religious books are published in the United Kingdom. Someone, somewhere, must be buying them.

Also, at the time of writing there are more than four hundred Christian bookshops in the country, and around seven thousand registered Christian book agents, most of whom are church bookstall managers. Apart from a very few giants with a turnover of £2000 a year, most may take only £100–£300. It is not the size that matters, but the need of the particular congregation or neighbourhood. One of the first things to do before starting up a bookstall, is to assess the local situation, which will determine the form your bookstall will take.

'But people in our area just don't read books,' you may complain. Don't despair. They read something, don't they? Newspapers? Magazines? Comics? Christian literature comes in many shapes and sizes.

What kinds of book?
A leaflet prepared for the guidance of bookstall managers, by Mowbrays, a major chain of Christian bookshops, lists the following categories:

> Baptism, Bibles, Bible stories, Biographies, Children's books, Christian conduct, Christian life, Church history, Church teaching, Communicants' manuals, Confirmation, Daily readings and meditation, Devotional, Doctrine, Ecumenical, Evangelism, Family life, Holy Communion, Laity training, Marriage, New Testaments in modern translations, Prayer, Sex questions, Science and religion, Social problems, Stewardship, Teaching of Jesus, Teenage religion, Worship, Youth prayers . . .

to which we could add novels, poetry, picture books, 'strip cartoon' presentation of Bible stories, as well as humorous cartoons, and many more. Potential customers who would find a conventional bound book daunting, may be induced to pick up an illustrated booklet which may meet their particular need at that moment. And don't forget the families. Parents who never read themselves, will read Bible stories to their children. Children's books are a good means of getting Christian literature into the home.

It is the bookstall manager's task to make his customers aware of what books are available, and to persuade them to read them.

The bookstall and the church

If your first thought in running a bookstall is to increase church funds, you can forget it. The properly managed bookstall should break even and it may well make a profit—but this will always be small.

The true role of the bookstall is as an extension of the church's pastoral ministry, and the wise minister will regard it as such and give it every encouragement. In one Anglican church, where the parochial church council works on a committee system, the bookstall manager is a member of the pastoral committee, along with the lay reader, the Sunday school manager and the missionary secretary. Wisely chosen and properly used, Christian literature can play a valuable part in evangelism and in building up the faithful—and increasingly also, these days, in pre-evangelism, creating a climate in which a person is prepared to think about the Christian faith. In all this, there needs to be co-operation and a good relationship between the bookstall manager and his minister.

It is, of course, essential to consult your minister, as well as your church council or other authoritative body, before you take any steps in the matter. Most ministers will welcome the idea of a bookstall, especially if someone else is prepared to take on the work of running it! However, any minister, quite rightly, will need to be convinced that you know exactly what you are doing, and that you are not going to let the church in for a fair amount of expenditure, only to drop the project at the first sign of discouragement—and there will be discouragements! You will need to impress him, not only with your knowledge of books, but with your awareness of the pastoral implications of your work, and with your ability to cope with practical matters such as keeping accounts. You must be prepared to consult him as to what books you will stock.

Some practical preliminaries

1. Site
Choosing the right site is important, and again this should be discussed well in advance with your minister and anyone else concerned. Three essentials to consider are:

i) *Accessibility*. Don't put your bookstall where people have to go out of their way to find it; or, at the other extreme, where it will cause a bottleneck and prevent people getting by. Just by the main church door may seem a good site—nobody can miss seeing it there— but if it causes a traffic hold-up you may create more ill-will than support.

Ideally, choose a place where people gather to chat after the service or meeting, where they have both room to move around and time to browse. And here one might mention another incidental use of the bookstall. Notice how some shy new member, trying to pluck up courage to speak to someone, will gravitate to the bookstall for something to do. Here is your opportunity to say a few welcoming words— as well as to sell them a book!

ii) *Lighting*. Be sure there is enough light for your customers both to notice the bookstall in the first place and to be able to examine the books easily. If there is not sufficient natural light, arrange for a spotlight to be installed.

iii) *Space*—both to display the books and to give your customers room to browse without blocking the view of other people. There is a complete chapter on Display later in this book.

2. Finance
If your supplier will not allow you credit at first— and he is unlikely to do so unless he knows you well—you will need to obtain a float from church funds. This could involve more money than you think, so plan carefully. You will need initially as

many as forty to fifty books to make a proper display and provide enough variety, and the price of books is rising rapidly.

Arrange with your church treasurer how this money will be repaid, and how your bills will be settled. Discuss also, at this stage, the procedure for recording your daily takings. Read carefully the section on accounting in chapter six and take your treasurer's advice.

Staffing
Even if you plan to look after the bookstall yourself, it is as well to recruit others who will help out in case of sickness, holidays or other commitments. You will find that running the bookstall can prove a great tie, particularly if you do not have a permanent lock-up fixture, and you have to set out and pack away your books at each session. You will always have to arrive early to open it up, and usually remain until everyone else has gone before closing down. It is helpful to have someone to share these duties.

With these preliminary arrangements completed, you are ready to start. But first, some words of warning.

Running a bookstall can be a hard slog. There will be days when you sell nothing at all. You will find yourself giving up a lunch hour or a Saturday morning to pick up a customer's urgent order. You will stagger under the weight of heavy parcels. You will spend more hours on the church premises than you thought possible, setting out books, arranging displays, attending to customers who always seem to wait until just before you pack up.

You will also have great fun. And a lot of satisfaction.

It is all worth it when the Sunday school child from a godless, bookless home, comes up to you and says,

'You know that story I bought, that story about Narnia? It isn't just a story, it's a proper book. It tells you something. I think it's saying something about God.

'Have you got another one like that?'

Check points
* Remember, a church bookstall is a ministry, not a means of making money.
* Size up your local situation.
* Consult your minister and/or church council.
* Do your homework. Understand what is involved.
* Choose a suitable site—accessible, well lit and roomy.
* Make suitable financial arrangements.
* Choose your helpers.
* Be prepared for hard work.
* Read the rest of this book!

2

How to start

How not to start

What you can *not* do is send off an order to a publisher and expect him to supply you with his products at a discount. Publishers do not normally allow trade discount to anyone other than a registered bookseller, and they will certainly not allow you credit.

A very few churches have large bookstalls with a high annual turnover, which have in effect achieved the status of bookshops. These are usually in cathedrals or other well-known churches on the tourist beat, which are able to keep the stall fully staffed every day throughout the week. They are in the fortunate position of being able to obtain their supplies at the full trade discount, usually thirty-five per cent.

At the other end of the scale, we have all seen those depressing, dingy tables at the back of country churches where a few tatty booklets and paperbacks repose amongst the dust along with out-of-date missionary magazines which nobody ever buys. These books were, as likely as not, bought at full price by some well-meaning vicar wanting to give his people the opportunity of reading, but nobody had either the time or the expertise to cope with a properly run bookstall.

The Book Agency scheme

The most efficient procedure, and the one which offers the most advantages to the average church, is to register with the Publishers Association as a Book Agent. This will enable you to obtain all the books you want (provided they are religious books) from a bookseller of your choice, at an agreed discount, usually ten per cent. You will not make much of a profit by this arrangement but, if you manage your bookstall wisely, you should not make a loss either. And assuming that your main motive is to get people to read Christian books, rather than to swell the church's funds, you will have achieved your object.

First choose your bookseller

If you are fortunate enough to have a Christian bookshop in your area which is willing to supply you, you are in the ideal situation. Otherwise you will have to weigh up the relative advantages and disadvantages of choosing either a local general bookseller, who may not stock a very wide range of Christian books, or a Christian bookshop which may be some distance away. In the latter case you can always order books by post, but this will rapidly eat up any discount you are allowed on the books themselves.

If you decide that you would prefer to deal through a Christian bookshop, and you know of none in your area, the Booksellers Association (see Appendix III) will always be glad to advise you of the nearest to your locality. Bear in mind that even Christian bookshops may be of different traditions, and an agent from, say, an evangelical church may not find the complete range of titles he wants in a catholic shop, or *vice versa*. This difference, however, is fast disappearing as Christians are more ready to read about and learn from, if not to agree with, each other's traditions.

The small general bookseller, with limited shelf space, may well decide that he cannot afford to cater for what he thinks is a minority taste, and will stock few if any religious books. Many larger shops have a 'religion and theology' section of sorts, though even these, unless the manager has a particular interest in this area, may limit their range to Bibles, prayer books and a few popular classics or paperbacks. However, no shrewd businessman will turn away good business, and if you can persuade a bookseller that you have a genuine outlet for Christian books he may agree to supply you.

There are signs that booksellers as a whole are becoming more aware of the sales potential of religious books. This is due to a large extent to such events as Christian Book Fortnight and other promotional efforts which have been organised with the aim of making the public aware of Christian books.

All booksellers should be aware of the opportunities these present, and encourage their Book Agents to participate.

If you do find that there are problems in registering with your local general bookshop, there is nothing to prevent you registering with two shops, or even three. Some Book Agents find this a useful arrangement. If your local shop does not have a particular title you want, you may be able to get it from a Christian bookshop further afield. However, many supplying booksellers stipulate a certain minimum amount which an agent must spend in their shop. This is reasonable, as you are involving your bookseller in a certain amount of extra work. Find out beforehand if the shop you wish to use makes any such stipulation, and decide whether the amount of business you expect to do will warrant the use of two suppliers.

Registering as a Book Agent
Having obtained the consent of your friendly bookseller, now is the time to apply to the Publishers Association (see Appendices) for your licence. A brief letter stating your desire to register as a Book Agent, and giving the name of the chosen bookseller, as well as the name and location of your church, is all that is needed. The PA will then send you a formal agreement, setting out the terms on which you will be allowed to operate (see Appendix II). A fee is charged, £5 plus VAT at the time of writing.

In effect, you are agreeing to purchase books only from your registered supplier, and not to sell at less than the full published price. You may find that from time to time publishers will mail agents with tempting 'special offers' of new books at attractive discounts for cash, to be obtained direct from the publisher concerned. This is contrary to the terms of your agency agreement.

Being a registered Book Agent brings with it several advantages. You will receive regular mailings from publishers, with news of their latest and forthcoming books. You are in a position to obtain professional advice from your supplying bookseller. It is, after all, in his interest to help you to sell as many books as possible. You also have the opportunity to attend conferences where you can meet other Book Agents and exchange ideas.

Choosing your basic stock

Once you receive your licence, you are in business and can place your first order. You will probably already have given some thought to your basic stock, and will have consulted both your bookseller and your minister. A few practical guidelines at this stage are:

1. Know how much you can spend.

Whether you have a float from your treasurer, or credit from your supplier, be careful to keep inside the limit. Don't over-invest in stock which may prove difficult to sell. It is unlikely at the start that your bookseller will allow you to take books on a 'sale or return' basis. One way round this might be to invite him to the opening occasion and to bring stocks of books himself. Other considerations apart, it would be good publicity for his shop, and might rate a paragraph in the local paper.

2. Know your potential customers.
Talk to them. Find out their reactions to the idea of a bookstall. Discover their interests, the kind of book, if any, they read for pleasure, the subject they want to learn more about. If there are several young families in your church, buy in a selection of children's books, and books about family relationships. If you have a lot of students, find out their particular concerns. Talk to the people whom you know to be reading Christian books already, and ask their advice.

3. Begin with paperbacks.
Apart from the obvious fact that, on a limited budget, you will get a greater variety of books this way, you will probably find that you have to educate your customers into spending out on books. They may not be in the habit of bringing much money with them when they come to church or to week-night meetings—apart from their offering, that is.

Pre-publicity
Several weeks before you plan to open your book-stall, begin to publicise it. The following are some suggestions.
1. Write an article for your church magazine.
2. Ask the leaders of various groups to allow you to talk to them about Christian literature. (This could

be a useful way of finding out what kind of books they would like you to stock.)

3. Send a letter (delivered by hand to save postage) to every member on the church register.

4. A week or two before the opening date, put leaflets in the pews listing some of the titles you will have on display.

5. Discuss with your minister the possibility of having a special Book Sunday to coincide with the opening, with special sermons on the importance of Christian reading.

Don't overdo it, though. It is suggested that you might use some, but not all, of the above methods. Aim to inform, but not to pressurise. Other people's enthusiasms can be excessively boring to those who do not happen to share them, and to overdo the publicity may be counter-productive. The message you need to get across to your customers is that the bookstall is there for their benefit, not for your own amusement; you must be willing to go at their pace, even if things move slowly at first. Be prepared for apathy, as well as interest.

The opening
It is as well to give some thought to the timing of your opening. Dates to avoid are the summer months, between June and August, when congregations tend to be low because of summer holidays. Early autumn, when most churches start up activities after a summer break, can be a good time. Better still is Christmas—but not too near to Christmas itself. A date in late November, when thoughts

of present-buying are beginning to make themselves felt, is a good time. Lent, also, can present a suitable occasion, when many churches encourage their members to make a point of reading a devotional book.

If you decide to tie-in your opening to Christian Book Fortnight, you can take advantage of the professionally produced posters, leaflets and other publicity material provided at a reasonable price by the organisers. It may be that other churches, or bookshops, in your area are organising special events, and this could give you another peg on which to hang your publicity.

Depending on your circumstances, you could arrange to make a major ceremony of your opening occasion, with perhaps (if your minister agrees) a visiting preacher connected with Christian literature, at the morning service. You might invite a well-known Christian author to be present to talk to customers and sign copies of his book. Or you may prefer to open quietly, with little more than an announcement from the minister that the bookstall will now be available after the service or meeting.

Whichever approach you choose, aim to make it clear that this is for everyone, and part of the on-going ministry of the church. This may perhaps best be done by having a short dedicatory ceremony, invoking God's blessing on the bookstall, its activities and its outreach.

Check points
* Find a bookseller who stocks the books you need and is willing to supply you.
* Apply to the Publishers Association for a Book Agent's licence.
* Plan your basic stock (see also chapter 3).
* Choose your opening date.
* Publicise.

3

Selecting your stock

When you come to place your first order, you may well be bewildered by the sheer number of titles available. How can you begin to know which to choose?

It helps to consider books in their various categories.

Bibles and New Testaments
It used to be said that every Christian should possess only one Bible—he should give the rest away. That was in the days when the Authorised Version was almost the only version in common use. During the last thirty years or so, there has been a plethora of new translations, and most Christians like to own two or three, at least.

In the 1940s we had the Revised Standard Version, and J. B. Phillips' masterly paraphrase of the New Testament. Then came the New English Bible, followed in rapid succession by the Jerusalem Bible, the Living Bible, the Good News Bible, and most recently the New International Version. There are also other less well-known modern translations, usually American, which your bookshop may have on its shelves.

Each of these versions has its particular advantages and drawbacks. If yours is a fairly small bookstall, you will not be able to stock them all. A compromise is always to keep in stock a cheap edition of each of the newest versions—either in paperback or in one of the inexpensive hardback 'schools' editions. This gives browsers a chance to sample the different translations, and you can then let them know what editions are available. You may find it useful to compile a price list, checking from time to time that the prices are correct—they have a habit of going up with each new printing.

The publishers of the main modern translations are:

Good News Bible—Collins; Bible Society
Jerusalem Bible—Darton, Longman and Todd; Eyre and Spottiswoode
Living Bible—Kingsway Publications
New English Bible—Oxford and Cambridge University Presses; Bible Society
New International Version—Hodder & Stoughton
J. B. Phillips—Collins (and Fount Paperbacks)

A useful Bible for study purposes is the Amplified Bible (Marshall, Morgan & Scott) which gives alternative renderings of certain words, to bring out particular nuances of meaning. It is also possible to buy Bibles, or parts of Bibles, in which several translations are printed in parallel columns, or some other device is used to compare the different versions. These are particularly useful for detailed Bible study. The ultimate is the *New Testament from 26 Translations*.

From time to time you will be asked for 'a proper Bible', by which the customer will mean the traditional leather-bound, India-paper volume. Unless he specifies a particular version, he is likely to mean the Authorised Version. But even traditional bindings have many variations, and you will find it useful to keep catalogues from the major Bible publishers so that your customer can decide for himself exactly what he wants. The Authorised Version, being Crown copyright, is only published in England by certain publishers. These are the Oxford and Cambridge University Presses, and Eyre and Spottiswoode. It is also published in Scotland by William Collins, and distributed by licence in England; and it is distributed by the Bible Society.

Some terms you may find useful in publishers' descriptions of Bibles are:

Text Bible—contains the text only, without references
Reference Bible—with references and notes, usually in a central column
Indexed Bible—enables the reader to find any book by means of a 'thumb index' in the page edges

India paper—very thin and light, but opaque, the thinnest paper available

Bible paper—slightly thicker and less luxurious than India, but still making a slim volume

Yapp—an overlapping cover to protect the edges of the book

Semi-yapp—narrower than yapp, but fulfilling the same purpose

Amethyst, Sapphire, Cameo, Turquoise, Ruby, etc.—type sizes, usually illustrated in the catalogue.

Besides Bibles and New Testaments, it is also possible to buy separate books of the Bible, or collections of books. These are often published in the form of attractive booklets, sometimes with photographic illustrations.

For those with poor eyesight, there are large print editions of the Gospels in the Good News Bible translation, published by the Bible Society. Some readers who cannot manage the type in normal Bibles, find a lectern Bible readable, though clumsy to handle. It is also possible to obtain the Bible on cassettes and the Torch Trust for the Blind (see Appendix iii) has portions in Braille and in large type.

Bible reading aids
The simplest of these are Bible-reading notes, either dated for daily use, or undated, which take the user through a planned programme of Bible reading, a short passage each day, with brief explanatory notes. These are produced for all ages and at all levels, by

the Scripture Union, the Bible Reading Fellowship, the International Bible Reading Association, as well as by various denominations. The Salvation Army's scheme, *The Soldier's Armoury*, is published in paperback format by Hodder and Stoughton, and is read far beyond the ranks of the Salvation Army.

Concordances and Bible dictionaries are useful study tools. The concordance is an alphabetically arranged word book giving the location of any Bible text by looking up the key word. A dictionary, as its name suggests, gives the meaning of the word; many Bible dictionaries also give a good deal of additional information, and are practically encyclopaedias. There are paperback and other cheap editions of concordances and dictionaries, some of them abridged versions of more weighty hardback volumes.

Comprehensive concordances, encyclopaedias and Bible handbooks, being large volumes, are generally more expensive, and you will probably not want to keep them in stock; with the possible exception of those designed for the family bookshelf, like the Lion *Handbook to the Bible*. It may be advisable to try out these more expensive books on a special occasion, perhaps on Bible Sunday, and obtain them on a 'sale or return' basis, rather than tie up money by keeping them permanently in stock. Once your customers know what is available, they can order them from you separately.

Commentaries, too, are best kept for special orders, except for the paperback one-volume commentaries, of which there are several available.

You should certainly have one or two books which provide a general introduction to the Bible, its history and its cultures, as well as those which help the reader to find his way about the Bible, and to understand its literary forms.

How-to books

These are often found in bookshops under the general heading of The Christian Life, and set out to answer all the questions that Christians, and would-be Christians, have been asking in every generation since Nicodemus wondered, 'How can a man be born again?' and the first disciples asked, 'Teach us how to pray.'

There are books to tell us how to make our prayer life more effective; how to witness to our faith; how to improve our marriage; how to bring up our family; how to cope with teenage problems; with middle age; with old age; how to face suffering or bereavement; to endure loneliness; how to adopt a Christian lifestyle (including suitable recipe books); how to be more feminine; even such things as how to lose weight in the cause of Christian witness!

While techniques can never supply the whole answer to the problems which plague us, they can give a great deal of help, as can the experiences of more mature Christians who have found their own way through these problems, and are willing to share their experiences.

Always keep a few how-to books in stock.

Christians in society

Sometimes overlapping with the previous category are books which deal with matters of social concern: race relations, the problems of industry, homosexuality, abortion, euthanasia, world poverty, conservation, etc.

While not everyone will want to go into these subjects in depth, they are questions which concern most of us at some level. Several publishers have produced booklets on social topics which can form the basis for group discussion, or provide an individual reader with food for thought.

Get to know what is available, and what may be particularly relevant to your own neighbourhood and congregation.

Wider horizons

The Bible-and-science debate still goes on, though less fiercely than it did a century ago. Many of us are so accustomed to the assumption that science undermines belief in God that it comes as a surprise to learn that many of our leading scientists in the fields of astronomy, physics and the natural sciences are committed Christians, and claim that their knowledge has reinforced, rather than undermined, their faith. Many of these are skilled popularisers, and are able to write about their subject at a level understood by the majority who are not experts. Archaeologists, too, are making discoveries which cast new light on our understanding of the Bible. Young Christians especially may be led to helpful books in these fields which can strengthen their faith in the face of possibly conflicting teaching at school or college.

Not always by established scientists are books which set out to refute pseudo-scientific best-sellers like *The Bermuda Triangle* or the writings of Erich von Däniken, or to find Christian explanations for, or arguments against, such phenomena as UFOs.

Sound teaching

When it comes to books of Christian doctrine, you may need to seek guidance from your minister regarding titles or authors within your particular church tradition. He may have strong ideas on the matter, since books sold on church premises may be assumed to reflect the teaching of that church. On the other hand, Christians of all traditions are becoming much more open to learn about their neighbours in other denominations, and if you are allowed a free choice you may find considerable interest among your church members in how other traditions—or even other religions—think and worship.

Encourage your minister to tell you in advance if he plans to preach a series of sermons, or run a Bible study or Lent course, on a particular point of doctrine, and ask him to recommend a suitable book or books to be read in that connection, so that you can have copies available at the appropriate time.

There are certain basic titles, like C. S. Lewis's *Mere Christianity* (Fount) or John Stott's *Basic Christianity* (IVP), which are acceptable within most traditions, and which are good introductory books for those on the fringe of the church. Don't reject standard books like those of C. S. Lewis on the grounds that most people must know them by now. There is always someone to whom they are a new discovery.

When it comes to more advanced theology, you will be more cautious. There will only be a few of your church members who read books in this category, and they will usually know exactly what they want. These are cases for special orders.

Devotional reading
You should have a steady sale for devotional books. These can include books of prayers or meditations, for personal use or for use in church or group worship. There are daily readings, of the *Through the Year with* . . . type, from the writings of a single author, or anthologies from many writers on a single devotional theme. There are modern translations of the writings of the great mystics, and of classics from earlier centuries such as *The Imitation of Christ*.

Books in this category available in large type editions include such modern classics as *Daily Light*, a compilation of Bible verses on daily themes; *My Utmost for His Highest*, again daily devotional readings, each based on a verse of Scripture; and Rita Snowdon's *Prayers in Later Life*. Older members of the church may be glad to know about these.

Also popular with older people, and with others, are the sort of 'pictorial meditation', in which photographs, illustrating or complementing a devotional text, play as much part as the words themselves in inducing a sense of worship.

Biographies

Not all Christian reading need be deeply earnest. Everyone likes reading about other people and there are numerous Christian biographies which are entertaining as well as uplifting. They come in great variety. A spot check in the biography section of a major Christian bookshop, just the titles on display, revealed up to 223 different titles in paperback editions. Subjects ranged from Augustine to astronauts, from Teresa of Avila to Mother Teresa of Calcutta, and included numerous testimonies of otherwise unknown Christians whose lives are examples of adventure or fortitude, sometimes of both—people who have learned to cope with suffering, people who have been liberated by Christ from a life of crime, or drug addiction, or bondage to the occult.

Through a good biography we can discover the human side of the greatest saints, and surprise touches of sanctity in the most ordinary of humans. For the great majority of people who lead quite ordinary lives, often with the feeling that most days are humdrum, Christian biographies can be an inspiration and, at the same time, enlarge our experience.

It is useful to have a selection of biographies and autobiographies to recommend to a customer who is looking for something fairly light, or to a fringe member for whom the relevance of Christianity in daily life is becoming a reality. The most frequently cited example of a book in this category, among several booksellers and bookstall managers, is Corrie Ten Boom's *The Hiding Place* (Hodder and Stoughton) and it has become a regular stock item in the majority of bookstalls.

Fiction

Christian fiction has had a bad name in the past: frequently there was some justification for the critical comments about 'poor writing' and the 'pill-in-the-jam' kind of plot in which the story is merely a vehicle for the message, usually to the detriment of both.

Perhaps this generally inadequate fictional writing, particularly noticeable among old-fashioned 'reward' books intended for prizes, discouraged many publishers from attempting to cater for the Christian fiction market; there are few catalogues in which Christian fiction has any real showing.

Yet there are some titles which have been consistently popular down the years, Charles M. Sheldon's *In His Steps* for instance and, more profoundly, John Bunyan's *Pilgrim's Progress* offered in dozens of editions in the original text as well as in simplified language.

There is a place for the Christian romantic novel and the publishers who have been producing a wide range of this kind of material for many years, Pickering & Inglis, include both American and British authors in their list. Don't despise this kind of fiction. You may well find people in your church, possibly older women, who like a good sentimental read which has the merit of a guaranteed clean plot with no sex or violence—a recommendation for many people these days.

When it comes to the novel as literature, it is not surprising that the best Christian novels are those written first and foremost as novels, and which perhaps were never consciously 'Christian' works. Notable in this field during the present century have been some of the novels by Morris West, Graham Greene, Alexander Solzhenitsyn, Rose Macaulay (every Anglican ought to read *The Towers of Trebizond*). Charles Williams has recently become popular again. C. S. Lewis is still a good read. His space trilogy claims wide attention even in the second decade of the actual space age, while perhaps not so well known is his more subtle *Till We Have Faces*.

There is the lively humour of the well-known writer of theology whose pseudonym, Neil Boyd, appears on such books as *Bless Me Father*; a section of the fiction range which again has a place on many bookstalls.

Have some fiction on display in the summer months and at other times when people are looking for light reading. Even if your usual supplier does not have them available, and you are therefore obliged to buy them in a general bookshop, they will add variety to your merchandise and may attract new customers.

Children's books

These come in most of the categories mentioned

above, with some more, and range from plastic picture books for tinies to novels for teens and sub-teens.

Probably in no other type of Christian literature have such advances been made, during recent years, in terms of quality. The full colour children's books published by, for instance, Lion and Scripture Union (now Ark books), compete in quality with the best on the secular market. It may be significant that both these companies have the declared aim of taking their books into the general bookshops. The Scripture Union-Ladybird tie-up is an example of the combination of Christian outreach with secular expertise. Perhaps this marks the beginning of the end of the ghetto mentality among Christian publishers, and in future we may see higher standards extending to other branches of specifically Christian publishing.

Quality colour books are necessarily expensive, though good value in terms of what they offer. While adults will always buy them for children, you need to stock cheaper books which the children can buy for themselves. There is a wide range of paperback fiction for children, varying in quality from the Narnia books downward. (Some people do not consider the Narnia books to be Christian, but most children are quick to spot the reality behind the allegory—perhaps a case of what has been called 'apprehending without comprehending'.)

Well written Bible stories always appeal, especially if the illustrations are good (they must be illustrated). There are some interesting pop-up

Bible story books in which a scene of the Ark, or of David and Goliath, or the Christmas manger, stand up from the page when the book is opened. Concordia's *Arch Books*, easy to handle and comfortably read at a sitting, are popular. They retell Bible stories in verse.

Children who are just learning to read enjoy the *Little Owl* books, small square eight-page booklets, and very colourful, with two or three words to a page. In the same format, but with more text and smaller type, are the *Luke Street* books, parables from Luke's Gospel, for those whose reading skills are slightly more advanced.

In the cheap and cheerful range are painting books, with biblical subjects or texts, which a child can buy for himself for a few pence. More expensive, but still in the do-it-yourself category, are cut-out cardboard models of Christmas cribs or other biblical scenes.

A recent trend in children's books, perhaps a result of selling into the secular market, is the one which tells an exciting story with no apparent Christian message, but with, on the last page, a few words pointing a Christian moral or a Christian parallel with the action of the characters, usually also quoting an appropriate scripture text. Collins' *Hippity Dog* and Scripture Union's *Rabbit* books are typical examples.

If you are nervous of choosing children's books, try taking one or two children to the shop with you, let them loose on the children's shelves, and note their reactions. You could learn a lot.

small single cards bearing a popular scripture passage (e.g. the Beatitudes, the Shepherd Psalm, the Ten Commandments), a prayer (e.g. the Prayer of St Francis), or a verse of poetry.

You can also buy these prayers and poems in larger sizes ready for framing, or already framed; wall plaques and religious pictures; crucifixes or plain wooden crosses; nativity figures etc.

For the children, there are even Bible card games and jig-saw puzzles.

Posters are popular, particularly with the young, and many Christian publishers are now producing them. It could be worth buying one or two to decorate your stall (or even, with permission, other parts of the church). People will soon start asking where they can obtain them.

Sunday selling
Selling on Sundays, and selling on church premises, are problems which concern many Christians. Objections raised usually come under one or more of three headings:

1. The actual act of buying and selling on Sunday is felt to be a wrong which is not outweighed by the pastoral aspects of the transaction, where Christian literature is involved. This view must be respected, and if there is a strong body of opinion in your church against a Sunday bookstall, you have to consider whether the bookstall can function in some other way—through group meetings or week-night meetings of the whole church, if you have them. It

Non-book books

For people who find all books, even paperbacks, intimidating, there are other forms of Christian literature.

Christian comics may sound a contradiction in terms. But you can buy comic strip versions of popular Christian books like *The Hiding Place* or *The Cross and the Switchblade*, printed on newsprint in bright colours, in a typical 'comic' format. There are also strip cartoon Bible stories, for reading by adults as well as children, this time in the more conventional paperback binding.

Some publishers produce magazine-type publications, highly illustrated, on a given theme, which can form the basis for group discussions, or be food for thought to an individual reader.

Small wire-stitched booklets, which alternate a colour photograph with Bible verses, poems, or short meditations, are produced by many publishers. Not much bigger than a greetings card, they can be slipped into an envelope and sent to a friend.

Books of humorous cartoons can point a message as well as raise a laugh. Mowbrays publish one a year, selected and introduced by a celebrity, from cartoons which have appeared in the press. Others contain collections of the work of a single artist— like the Brother Barnabas books, or Fiddy's and Iain Reid's *Tramps*. A warning about these, though. Customers tend to leaf through them at the bookstall, have a good laugh, and go away without buying!

Finally in this section we may mention music

books—song books, arrangements of Christian music for guitar, and so on.

All these things can serve as an introduction to the wider field of Christian literature.

Finding out
How can you discover what books are available?

1. First, and most obviously, by browsing round the shelves of your book supplier. If it is a Christian bookshop, there will be a large and representative selection for you to choose from. Don't just look at the titles; take time to pick them up and sample them. Ask the advice of your bookseller. Make an appointment with him if you want a long discussion, to be sure you are not encroaching on his time.

2. Study the book advertisements and reviews in the Christian press. If you do not regularly read a Christian newspaper or magazine, then you should certainly start now. Every Christian needs to be well informed about church affairs (see Appendix IV). You may find some of the major denominational papers in the reading room of your local library, and it is worth looking regularly at their book pages. Many of them have special book numbers in Lent and before Christmas.

3. SPCK publish *News and Views*, a broadsheet devoted to books, which appears as an inset in the major church newspapers. This is published three times a year, in Lent, June and November. It lists

a selection of forthcoming books, as well as carrying advertisements from most of the major religious publishers.

4. *Religion and Theology*, published annually as a paperback by SCM Press, lists books under various categories. This concentrates, as its title suggests, mainly on academic books, but it is a useful source of information in this field.

5. *The Bookseller* is the weekly publication of the book trade. Your local library is sure to have a copy, and will be glad to let you look at it. It will be kept at the main desk rather than in the reading room, and you must ask for it specially. It carries news of all that is going on in the book trade, and also lists at the back all books published during the current week. Since it covers the whole book trade, its use as a source of specialist information is somewhat limited. However, it has a paperback feature once a month, where you will find current Christian publications mentioned alongside the latest popular mass-market books.

You should certainly make a point of seeing the Export issues, which are published in February and August. These are bumper numbers in which publishers take the opportunity to publicise all their forthcoming books for the next six months. Consult the section on Religion and Theology. Take a notebook and pencil with you, and write down details of everything you think will be of interest to you.

6. Church bookstall managers have their own publications, *A Bookstalls Newsletter*. Besides carrying news of books, and publishers' advertisements, this also has items from bookstalls and bookshops all over the country. Though published privately, it is run in close association with the Christian Bookstall Managers Association (see Appendix III).

7. Book Agents registered with the Publishers' Association receive regular mailings, which enclose relevant leaflets, catalogues from publishers, newsletters and other publicity material.

8. It is worthwhile asking to be put on the mailing list of selected publishers who are most likely to be of interest to you. You should then receive their catalogues regularly.

9. Some bookshops and suppliers, serving a large number of agents, compile their own catalogues of recommended books.

10. To track down a book which has been published for some time, or books by a given author, consult *British Books in Print*; a complete record of books available in Britain, with publisher and price. It is published annually, in two fat volumes, under Title and Author respectively. Your public library will have it, and so, probably, will your bookseller. The information it contains is also available on microfiche, issued monthly.

11. *Paperbacks in Print* performs the same function as the above, for paperbacks only.

12. The *British National Bibliography* catalogues everything that has been published in Britain since 1950, under subject as well as under author and title. Ask to see it at your local library.

Check points
* Think before you buy.
* Choose a balanced selection.
* Have something for everybody—non-readers as well.
* If you don't know—find out.

4

Display—Fixtures and Fittings

The kind of furniture you provide for your bookstall will depend to some extent on when, where and how it is most likely to be used.

If you plan to open it only on Sundays, or at week-night services, a permanent fixture in some central spot convenient of access is probably your best choice.

You may, however, wish to make it available to group meetings, perhaps in smaller church rooms, perhaps in private homes. In this case you will do well to think of something more portable.

Another matter for consideration is whether you will be able to leave the books on permanent display, or will have to pack them away when the stall is not in use. Sadly, few churches are able to remain open during the week nowadays, but if your church door is left unlocked, you will be asking for trouble if you leave an open bookstall unattended.

You will also take into account how much money you have to spend, whether you are able to purchase ready-made display stands, or must make do with whatever is available.

On a shoestring
The most basic piece of equipment is a table covered with a cloth.

If you are running on a shoestring, this may be all you can manage, but it can be very effective. Choose a strong colour, not too bright, which will attract attention to the stall and also set off the covers of the books. Avoid patterned material, or anything that looks too obviously like a tablecloth! If a table is the only furniture, and no cupboard space can be found, you will probably have to store your books in cardboard boxes. By having the cloth sufficiently large to hang down to the floor in front, you can stow away your boxes and any other paraphernalia under the table out of sight.

An extra dimension can be added to your display by building up a step at the back of the table (under

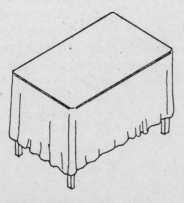

the cloth), using blocks of wood, bricks, or even other books.

Use the wall behind the table to display informative notices, posters, leaflets or spare book covers which you may be able to obtain from publishers (though they are not so free with these as they were in the past). If you push the table back firmly against the wall, you can also use it to prop up books in the back row of your display.

Display books 'face on' wherever possible—that is, with the front of the book facing the customer—and vertically, rather than lying flat. Even a paperback will stand up vertically without support if it is slightly opened.

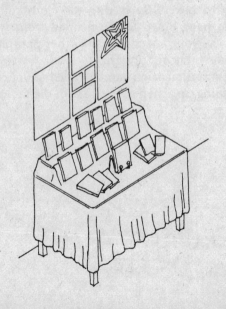

Publishers sometimes produce special display kits as part of their promotion material for a new title or series. It is worth asking your bookseller about these, if you think you can make good use of them.

With the exercise of a little ingenuity, there are many things you can do which need not cost you anything.

Get into the habit of looking out for items which can be used to help your display:

A plastic plate rack from the kitchen can be used to hold several paperbacks.

The gilt-paper covered lid of a chocolate box can hold a selection of miniature books for children.

An effective display of newspapers and magazines can be hung with clothes pegs from a line of coloured string.

A cardboard carton covered with wallpaper can make a 'dump bin' for second-hand books, in which customers are encouraged to rummage.

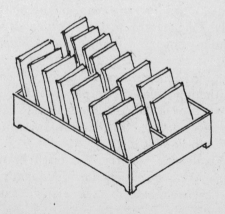

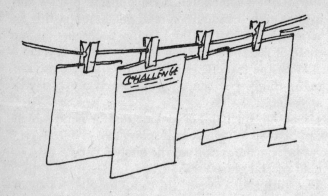

Labels and price tickets can be cut from the coloured parts of cardboard cartons.

On the cheap
So far, this display would cost practically nothing. With a small further expenditure, you can buy a piece of pegboard to stand at the back of the table. Special fittings for this can be obtained fairly cheaply. This gives your stall a vertical as well as a horizontal dimension, which immediately adds interest.

Paint the pegboard a colour which will effectively set off the items you are displaying. If you have a coloured cover to the table itself, a white backboard can be very effective. Wash it down occasionally to prevent it becoming grubby.

Cheap display material can often be obtained from shops that are closing down. A quantity of wire stands, each suitable to take a single book, was acquired in this way for 1p each. Given a spray with gold paint, they made a very smart addition to the bookstall furniture.

You may well be able to acquire display shelves or other large items in this way.

Do-it-yourself

If you are a good carpenter, or if you have a skilled handyman in the congregation who can be persuaded to help, you can produce display furniture to suit your individual requirements. We offer here some suggestions that have been found effective. These include—

1. Portable folding stands, useful if you are selling books at group meetings.

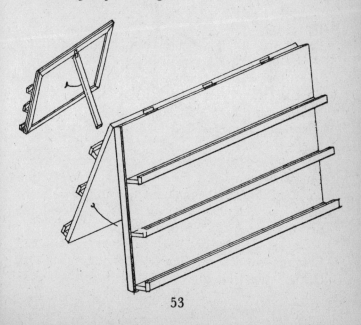

2. Display racks for standing on a table or flat surface.

3. Racks which fit on a wall, useful if you are limited for space.

4. Free-standing racks.

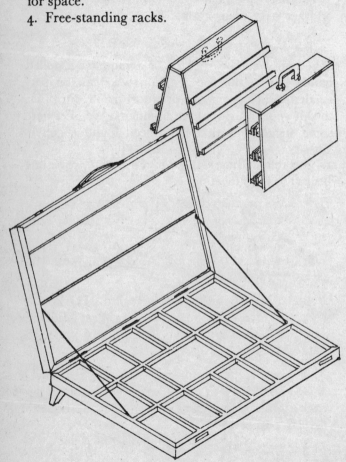

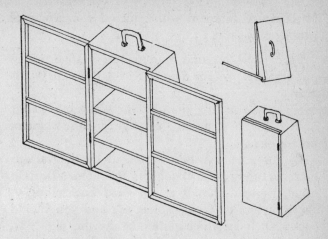

If you are buying
There are manufacturers of shop fittings who specialise in producing display racks suitable for bookstalls. Among these are:

Point Eight Ltd., Hope Street, Dudley, West Midlands, DY2 8RS.

Modern Merchandising Services Ltd., PO Box 17, Vicarage Street, Oldbury, Warley, West Midlands B68 8HG (their equipment is marketed under the name Modal).

E. P. Joseph Ltd., Supremacy House, Hurstwood Road, London NW11 0AR manufacture small perspex stands each capable of holding one book for display purposes.

M plus One, C. & J. Murrell Ltd, Field Road, Mildenhall, Suffolk, IP28 7AR produce a wide range of display equipment which includes a variety of wire display units.

From time to time manufacturers advertise in publications like *The Bookseller* or *A Bookstalls Newsletter*.

If you see just the kind of thing you want in your high street shop, ask the manager for the name of his supplier.

Explore the possibilities offered by the various manufacturers of shelving for the home. Bear in mind, though, that it is not good bookselling to show shelves of books 'spine on', and you should choose shelving which allows the showing of face on displays, by means of sloping shelves or other devices.

Some general rules for display

1. All items should be accessible. Customers must be able to pick up and examine the books. This means children as well—keep children's book low; but keep an eye on inquisitive toddlers.

2. Make sure that all prices are easily seen. Though most paperbacks carry the price on the back, many people do not realise this, especially if they are not familiar with books. Use labels and price tickets where necessary, but avoid the kind of stick-on label that does not easily peel off.

3. Don't have elaborate displays that collapse if a book is removed. Nothing scares customers off quicker!

4. Discover the optimum display points by watching which books are habitually picked up. On a vertical stand, it was noticed that it was not the books at eye level, but those in the row immediately *below* eye level, which regularly caught the attention.

5. Keep books of a similar kind together. A customer looking for books on prayer, for instance, does not want to have to hunt through the whole display before discovering what is required.

6. Make different displays for different occasions—in summer, feature novels, biographies etc. 'for holiday reading'; in Lent, devotional books, or a tie-in with the church's Lent study course; at Christmas, books suitable for gifts; for family services, children's books and books about family life.

7. Keep the display tidy. Keep an eye on it during a selling session, straighten any books when they

are left crooked, or replace any that have been moved out of place—but wait tactfully until the customer responsible has moved away!

8. Keep the books covered when the stall is not in use. If you do not have any means of locking them away, at least cover them with a sheet of polythene, to prevent dust collecting.

9. If books do become shop-soiled, remove them from display, and either keep them until you hold a sale, or put them in the second-hand section, if you have one.

Check points
* Use display to make buying easier.
* Attract, don't intimidate.
* Keep it simple.
* You don't need to spend a lot to make a good display.
* Use your imagination.

5

Selling

You will already have discovered that the duties of a bookstall manager include more than simply selling books. They involve such things as stock control, regular ordering of new supplies, knowing what to order, and keeping accounts. You do not need to be expert in all these matters, but you must know where to go for help if you need it. You will also find that you tend to become regarded as the resident specialist in all matters related to books, and you may be expected to answer questions which have nothing to do with the bookstall as such.

Your helpers, too, should be people who are genuinely interested in books, or their enthusiasm may quickly wane. Make sure they know from the start exactly what they are letting themselves in for. Arrange a regular duty rota, so that there is no misunderstanding about whose turn it is. But however much assistance you have, you remain the manager, and it is you who must take the final responsibility.

Hard sell and soft sell

Unlike most salesmen, you are not in this primarily to make money. Therefore it is not your job to pressurise people into buying against their will. An example of the hard sell is the enterprising bookstall manager who placed a copy of a new Bible translation on every seat in the church, with a note inviting the occupant to purchase it after the service. He sold a lot of copies, and greatly improved his turnover. One wonders, though, how many of the buyers, on reflection, regretted having been pushed into it, and resolved to avoid the bookstall in future.

But don't go to the other extreme and sit waiting for customers to flock to you of their own accord. It is part of your job to make them aware of their need.

First of all, make sure that people know you are there! A reminder from the minister when he is giving out the notices is useful, though if it happens every Sunday, people will cease to hear it. Persuade him to vary his approach. An oft-repeated exhortation to buy a book 'to help you in your Christian life' may be worthy, but it is hardly exciting.

Besides these verbal announcements, try putting up a notice by the main door for people to see as they leave the church. Occasionally put a leaflet in the pews. Arrange a small selection of books on a table near the exit door, with a notice to the effect that these and other titles are on sale, and where. Vary your approach.

Paradoxically, it has been found helpful to close down for a while, perhaps in the month of August. People who have taken the bookstall for granted as part of the furniture, soon notice if you are not there. When you start up again, perhaps with some fresh, specially announced attraction, they will be the more likely to come along and see what you have on offer.

Knowing your customers—and your stock
You have made your presence known. You have attracted customers to your bookstall. All you have to do is to sell them a book.

How you do this will vary with every customer and every book sold. It is a technique you will never stop learning. Your task is to encourage the timid, to advise the ignorant and to serve everybody. You have to learn to distinguish the genuine browser (who probably does not want to be interrupted) from the uncertain customer (who does). You have to know how tactfully to dissuade a customer from buying something totally unsuitable, while at the same time discovering and recommending the book which he really needs.

This involves a lot of background reading on your part. You must know your stock, and be able to tell customers what any book is about, what line it takes, something about the author. You do not actually have to read every book all the way through. You can often gather a good deal about it from the Introduction, or the first or last chapter.

Handling the money
Start off each selling session with a good supply of change. Note the exact amount there is in the till.

61

Some bookstalls function quite satisfactorily by simply leaving a box or some other receptacle, with a notice inviting customers to leave the price of their book and take change if necessary. Presumably most churchgoers are honest, and thefts of money, or taking a book without payment, do not normally occur. This is not, however, a very efficient way of working if you are keeping strict records of your stock and money. There is always the temptation, perhaps to a child, to cheat, and even the most honest customers are not immune from making a genuine mistake.

If you do use this method, keep a frequent eye on the till. Remove any notes as they appear, and keep them in a separate purse or container.

On the whole, it is wiser to handle the money yourself. If you are one of those people not too good at mental arithmetic, the safest way of giving the correct change is to state firmly the price of the book, then count out the change audibly when handing it to the customer, thus:

'One pound twenty-five; and five is thirty, forty, fifty. Two pounds.'

That way both you and your customer are satisfied that the amount is correct.

Book Tokens

From time to time, customers may ask to pay in book tokens. You will have to arrange with your supplying bookseller if this is acceptable. If you pay the bills in person, it may well be feasible. If you pass bills to your church treasurer for payment, book tokens could cause too many complications.

Buy now, pay later
It is not wise to make a practice of allowing people to take away books with a promise to 'pay next week'. Just as the most upright of characters tend to develop amnesia over returning a book they have borrowed, so they can become equally absent-minded when it comes to paying for one they have bought. If a customer has no money on him, offer to put the book on one side till next time.

If you do decide to allow credit, write down details of the debt in a notebook kept for the purpose, and don't be squeamish about chasing up the person concerned— even if it does happen to be the vicar! The best system is to have one of those duplicate order books where the top copy is torn off and given to the customer, while you retain the carbon. When the debt is paid, enter the date and the amount on your copy, and get the customer to sign it. That way any mistakes or unpleasantness are avoided.

Paying by instalments
While not recommended as a general practice, this can work well with children. A child who very much wants a particular book, perhaps a Bible, and is prepared to save up for it, can be encouraged to bring a little money every week. The money is entered in your notebook, so that the child can see the total, and 'his' book is kept on one side for him until he has paid for it. Always encourage a child

who really wants to own a book. You could be starting him on a habit of good reading for life.

Book-of-the-month

A way of attracting new readers, who may be a little uncertain when it comes to making a choice, is to feature a Book-of-the-month, with a special display, and perhaps a review in the church magazine, and a plug from the pulpit. This can be an excellent means of encouraging systematic reading in a congregation not very used to books. A display of several copies of the same title makes people more willing to buy, as does the knowledge that several others are doing the same. You may consider that once a month is too frequent to do this. In that case you could feature a 'summer special', 'Christmas special', 'Lent special', etc.

Book club

This is an adaptation of the above process, with the advantage that you have some indication in advance of how many copies you will need to order. It works on the same principle, in a small way, as the

commercial book clubs, in that members undertake to buy six or eight selected titles each year. This is a scheme in which the instalment method can be used with effect, club members paying a fixed amount weekly throughout the year. A lot of careful paperwork is involved, but a club of this sort has been proved to attract new readers.

The book club scheme has been used with great success by a church in Essex. On the other hand, when tried in a south London church it dropped like a stone. Like everything about running a bookstall, it is a matter of getting to know what will, and what will not, go down with your particular congregation.

Selling at group meetings
Besides the main occasions when the larger numbers are present, Sunday services and church meetings such as the mid-week Bible study or prayer meeting, you may find it worthwhile to have books on sale at group meetings. These may take place in private houses, or in other places away from the church premises; or they may be in small rooms apart from the church or church hall where your bookstall is situated.

Clearly it will not be possible to move your entire stock from place to place. A small portable bookstall, such as that described on page 53, or even just a cardboard box, packed with a suitable selection of books, should suffice.

Unless you are prepared to undertake a lot of extra duty, you should arrange with one particular member of the group to be responsible for sales. Insist that a careful record is made of every book sold, and of the amount of money taken, and ensure that the money is handed to you after every session. Keep a special notebook for this purpose, one for each group, and if the system fails and records are not kept, withdraw the privilege of the bookstall! It is essential that you keep control of all selling processes.

It may be as well to have the bookstall at group meetings only once a month. So long as it is regular, people will know when to expect it.

Special orders

Make it known that you are always prepared to take orders for any book you do not have currently in stock. If you are not familiar with the book requested, be sure to make a note of the exact title, author, and if possible, the publisher. Establish whether the customer wants a paperback or hard-back edition (if both are available), and if he has some idea of the price.

Above all, be sure that the customer actually wants to *buy* the book. Many a bookstall manager has been known to buy in, at some inconvenience and perhaps expense, a particular book in respose to the question, 'Have you got a copy of —?' only to be told when he produces it, 'Oh, I didn't actually want to *buy* it, I just wanted to have a look at it!'

Find out how urgently the book is required. Your customer may be prepared to wait until your next stocking-up visit to your supplier. If he wants it quickly, you must be prepared to make a special trip to the bookshop to get it—this is just one of the hazards of the job! If your supplier does not have that title available, buy it at full price from some other shop, if necessary, rather than keep your customer waiting.

Your bookseller will always order in a special book for you from the publishers. This may well take time, though, and your customer should be made aware of this.

You will soon establish a regular clientele for special orders, quite likely including your minister. These people usually know exactly what they want, and are glad to use the bookstall as a convenient means of obtaining it. Their orders will often be for more expensive books, and could account for a high proportion of your turnover. Keep a section of the bookstall for special orders, with a named slip in each book, to be collected by the person concerned. Other people will glance at them and perhaps, who knows, be encouraged to order a copy for themselves.

It is worthwhile building up a relationship with regular special order customers, who will usually be only too happy to talk books with you. Let them browse through your publishers' catalogues, and ask their advice on other titles you might stock.

Church supplies
The Book Agent's licence is not designed to allow churches to purchase bulk supplies at a discount. However, there is nothing to stop you buying hymn

books, prayer books or missals, Bibles for the pews or Sunday school materials, provided you do not pass on the discount to your church. Such orders will nicely swell your bookstall account, and will save your minister or other church officials a good deal of work. Your bookseller, too, will doubtless welcome a large order represented by these books.

Special occasions

There will be occasions when you will want to make a special display of books which are not normally kept in stock. It may be a church mission, a visiting preacher who is also a well-known author, or you may simply want to lay in some extra stock before Christmas. If you have a good relationship with your supplying bookseller, he will be glad to let you have extra books on a sale or return basis. Do give him plenty of advance warning, however, and do him the courtesy of returning unsold stock as soon as possible after the occasion.

This leads us to one or two technical terms you will come across in the bookselling business.

On sale or return

There are two terms used in the trade for this arrangement. 'On sale' means that the books are literally 'on sale or return'. All books returned unsold from that particular order are credited to the customer. 'See safe' means that the supplier will replace any unsold copies with other goods to the same value.

Any books returned to your bookseller must of

course be in mint condition. He is within his rights to refuse to accept any well-handled or dog-eared copies.

Net and non-net
When resale price maintenance was abolished on most commodities in 1962, the Publishers Association fought a hard legal battle to have it retained on books. It was successfully argued that, if large stores or chain stores were to undercut prices, not only would many bookshops go out of business, but publishers would no longer be able financially to produce quality books with a restricted print run. The result would be to flood the market with poor quality books, to the detriment of the educational and cultural standards of the nation.

Books are therefore the only commodity still subject to a controlled retail price. Both publishers and booksellers argue about the merits of this situation. There is a let-out, however. Books marked with a 'net' price (e.g. £1·25 net), may not be sold below that price. But some publishers, including some leading Christian publishers, do omit the word 'net', and this *may* indicate that they are 'non-net' books—i.e. they can be sold at a reduced rate. Check with your bookseller!

In practice, this will not affect you very much since your rate of profit will depend on the price at which your supplier sells to you. Technically, it could make a difference if you decided to have a sale of old stock.

Non-net books frequently do not have the price

printed on the cover, but it is pencilled inside the book itself, or sometimes omitted altogether. You should always be sure that the books you sell are marked with the price. Check against your invoice, or check back with your bookseller, if you are not sure.

VAT

At the time of writing, books are zero-rated for VAT. Other things you may sell are not. As the law stands at present, your turnover will not in all probability bring you into the class where you will be liable for VAT—if it does, you should be functioning as a shop rather than an agency! But the situation may change, and should be watched. When in doubt, consult your bookseller.

Book sale

Because of the Net Book Agreement (see above), you cannot simply hold a sale and reduce your prices whenever you feel like it. The National Book Sale which happens throughout the book trade every year, is the outcome of special agreements between publishers and booksellers and is a carefully regulated means for both parties to get rid of their surplus stock. One of the rules provides that no item may be offered for sale at more than the price (less discount) at which it was purchased from the publisher. This prevents shops buying in books specially for the sale, and still making a small profit. You may not reduce the price of new books unless you have had them in stock for more than twelve months, and then, strictly speaking, only with the permission of the publisher. When in doubt, consult your bookseller. In practice, breaches of this rule are usually winked at where only a few copies are concerned, particularly if the books have become tatty. A book sale is in fact about the only way (short of throwing them away) of getting rid of your soiled or damaged stock, and it is a good way of attracting new customers.

Second-hand books

Everybody likes a bargain, and a box or display of 'bargain books' is always an attraction. This section of your bookstall need cost you little or nothing. Members of the congregation will usually be quite happy to donate books they have finished with, in the knowledge that they will be recycled to be of use to someone else. Subject to the provisos mentioned above, casualties of the main part of the bookstall may end up here too—those copies which have been hard to get rid of and have become dog-eared with much handling. Marked down to half their original price, they will miraculously be snapped up, probably by the very people who have been responsible for their shabbiness! But at least you will have got rid of them.

Newspapers and magazines

You do not need to be a book agent to obtain newspapers and magazines. These you will obtain direct from the publishers, who offer a discount on quantities. Most of the recognised church denominations have a regular publication and there are also many non-denominational journals and magazines (a list is given in Appendix iv).

Being an agent for a weekly newspaper poses some problems. Most of these publish on Thursdays or Fridays. If the weekly order is late in delivery, the papers may not be there for the following Sunday, and a whole week's issue could be lost to the customers. This is particularly liable to happen if the order is posted to the agent's home. Placing an order through a local newsagent could be safer. In this case you would lose your discount, but whether this consideration is more important than the service you are offering to church members is something you must weigh up for yourself. This arrangement also involves you, or somebody else, in the inconvenience of collecting them every Saturday.

Monthly publications do not pose the same problems. You may well try ordering a few copies over and above your firm orders and sell them alongside your books.

Bible Reading Notes
A similar system can be used to distribute Bible reading notes, if your church does not already have an agent looking after that duty.

Come-ons
The things mentioned in this section are not books at all, but are aimed at attracting to your bookstall customers who would not come to it in the usual way.

In the early 1970s, at the height of the 'Jesus Movement', there was a craze, originating in America, for what became known irreverently to the trade as 'Jesus junk'—badges, car stickers ('Honk if you love Jesus'), tee shirts bearing slogans like 'Get turned on to Jesus', gaudy religious 'jewellery', and much else. These by-products of the hippy era were mostly junk, and of dubious value as a witness to the wearer's faith. The worst examples have now, fortunately, disappeared from the market, but the ideas have survived, to be taken up by talented designers. Most Christian bookshops now stock items like lapel badges, brooches or pendants with a Christian motif (most popular are small crosses, a stylised fish design, or a dove).

You can buy Christian stationery, in the form of writing paper, Notelets or greeting cards bearing Scripture texts; calendars and diaries; even paper table napkins and place mats.

Some companies produce pictorial cards which are almost booklets, printed with short prayers and words of comfort to send to the sick or the bereaved. The Bible Society has selections of Bible verses in a modern translation, attractively presented in a greetings card format.

A word of warning about Christmas cards, Advent calendars and other seasonal items. Don't overstock, or you will be stuck with them for a whole year before you can put them on sale again. It is better to disappoint some customers than to overstock heavily.

Useful and inexpensive items are bookmarks or

can be done, though it needs careful organisation. There are church bookstalls which, in spite of not selling on Sundays, still have an annual turnover of several hundred pounds.

A system by which people can look at the books on Sunday, and even choose one and take it away, but actually pay for it later in the week, is one way of overcoming this problem. Whether you use it or not will depend on whether you consider the act of selling consists in the handing over of the money, or whether it involves the whole process of examining and selecting the goods purchased.

2. The presence of the bookstall could be said to involve the manager in working on Sunday. The same might be said of the sidesmen who hand out the hymn books, the Sunday school teachers, or even the minister. However, there may be a distinction to be made between these duties and the avoidable work of selling.

Some define 'work' as carrying on the same activity as one is paid to do during the week. Thus a bookstall manager who is by profession a bookseller, or a shop assistant, could be said to be involved in work, whereas if he were an architect or a gardener, this would not be the case. This again is a matter for your own conscience, and the policy of your church.

3. Selling books in the church itself, rather than in a church hall or even in an entrance lobby, causes uneasiness to many who call to mind the incident of the cleansing of the Temple—'You have made my

Father's house a den of thieves.' For this reason many churches prefer to site the bookstall in the vestibule, or in the church hall, so that the church premises may not be defiled—though, as Timothy Dudley Smith has pointed out, the difference between placing in the offertory plate money to heat the church and paying for a book 'which will help to warm, not the body, but the heart', is a fine one.

It is important that the presence of a bookstall should not give offence to church members, and any objections on the grounds of conscience should be given serious consideration.

Check points
* Publicise, but be informative, not boring.
* Be available, but not aggressive.
* Know your customers.
* Know your stock.
* Handle money responsibly.
* Experiment with new ways of selling.
* Learn the rules of bookselling—and keep them!
* Aim to attract non-readers.
* Be sensitive to the principles of other church members.

6

Paper work

You cannot run an efficient bookstall without getting involved in a fair amount of paper work. It is absolutely essential that careful accounts be kept of all the money transactions; and, though not essential, advisable, that you have some system of stock control.

Daily records
The basis for both accounting and stock control is the daily record of sales, which should be strictly maintained by all who are involved in selling from the bookstall, including those responsible for selling at group meetings. These latter can most usefully enter their records in a duplicate invoice book which enables the top copy to be torn off and given to the bookstall manager, while the carbon copy is retained. The manager can then transfer the information to his own records.

All that you need is a simple cash book, with columns for date, transaction and money taken.

Your page for any given day would look like this:

Date		£	p
22.7	Float	1	73
	2 Ladybirds		48
	1 Cross & Switchblade	1	25
	1 NEB	2	50
	3 Little Owls		30
	1 Ladybird (from Wives' Group)		24
	1 Christian Family (from Wives' Group)	1	25
	2 Arch Books		70
		6	72
	Plus float	1	73
		8	45
	Paid in	7	00
	Cash float C/fwd	1	45

Stock control

Using the daily sales record as a basis, keeping control of stock is a fairly simple matter.

You need a looseleaf notebook, or card index, with a separate page for each title, or for a series if the books are uniform and bought in quantity rather than per title.

Rule the page into three main columns. Head the first *Copies bought*, the second *Total stock*, and the third *Copies sold*. Each column is then subdivided into two, with a space for the date and a space for a figure.

Head each page with the title of the book, and the price, which should be changed as the price goes up with a new printing, and a note made of the date of the change of price.

When you receive an order from your supplier, the first thing to do is to check the books against the invoice. Having done this, you then enter each individual title on the relevant page, in the *copies bought* column, and adjust the *total* column.

At the end of each day's selling, note the appropriate figure in the *copies sold* column, and again adjust the total.

Below is a sample record for an imaginary children's series called 'Minnows'.

MINNOW BOOKS – PRICE 30p (Mar '79)

Date	Bought	Stock	Sales
1.1.79	—	5	
7.1	—	2	3
11.1	12	14	—
14.1	—	13	1
28.1	—	12	1
4.2	—	7	5
4.3	—	1	6
9.3	12	13	

This record gives you a lot of useful information:

1. You can see at a glance how many copies you have in stock.

2. You can see the sales pattern (clearly you sell more copies on the first Sunday of the month, which is a family service).

3. It indicates that you could increase the number of copies purchased, perhaps buying more copies less frequently.

4. It can tell you whether sales have dropped off since a price increase, a possible guide in ordering similar series.

Likewise, this system warns you of the titles which are slow sellers, shows up which are not moving at all, and tells you whether they have been in stock long enough to qualify for a price reduction (see p. 70).

Comparison of various titles will show you what kinds of books are most popular, which lines could do with a little extra promotion, and which should be dropped altogether.

The system also acts as a double check when it comes to stock-taking.

Dead stock

If you have titles that show no sign of movement, there is no point in keeping them exposed for sale week by week. It is not a good advertisement for your regular customers to see the same titles always on display, getting shabbier and shabbier.

Apart from writing off your mistakes completely and throwing them away (which you may have to do as a last resort), there are various ways of dealing with them.

1. Try withdrawing them from sale for a while and bringing them back again when you hope everyone will have forgotten about them. An occasion when you expect a number of visitors, such as a guest service, or an anniversary, may be a suitable occasion.

2. Reduce the price and put them in your next sale (see p. 70).

3. Contact a neighbouring church, possibly of a different tradition, and offer to swap some of your dead stock for theirs. Quite often a book which won't sell in one church will find a ready buyer in another.

Stock-taking
This must be done at the end of every financial year.

Contrary to what many people think, the object is to establish the actual value, not the retail value, of your stock. You should therefore deduct from the face value of a book or other item the discount you were allowed on it (usually ten per cent). A further amount may be deducted for depreciation. A well-known bookseller recommends that books bought during the past year should be depreciated by five per cent, those bought more than a year previously, by twelve and a half per cent, and that after more than two years they should be written off.

It does not follow that you must immediately reduce the selling price on items marked down in this way. You can continue to offer them for sale at the full price, but the chances are they will eventually end up in a sale or in your second-hand section.

The value of your stock is important in presenting your annual accounts.

Accounts

If you are really hopeless at figures, you had better arrange for your church treasurer to keep your bookstall accounts. All you need to do then is to pass on to him all the information regarding expenditure:

1. All invoices.

2. A note of any purchases made out of cash takings, with a dated receipt.

3. A note of any purchases made on behalf of other church departments, where cash has not actually changed hands, thus:

> Please transfer to bookstall account from Sunday school account:
> Payment for 12 Bibles @ £2.50   30.00
> _____

>   (signed)   (date)

4. A note of any personal expenses you have incurred.

You also, of course, pass over to the treasurer the money for banking.

An advantage of passing your accounts through the church accounts in this way is that you can go temporarily into the red without undue complications—though you will not be popular if you end the year with a deficit.

However, we strongly recommend that every bookstall be run as a separate enterprise, with its own bank account.

Recording income and expenditure
Even if your treasurer does keep the official accounts, you will still need to keep track of the money you handle, for your own information.

If you have been keeping daily sales records, this is simply done. Use facing pages of an ordinary cash book. On the left-hand page record all expenditure, including invoices, any cash purchases, and incidental expenses. On the right-hand page, enter your daily takings, which you will get from your daily sales record.

It is important to record your incidental expenses, even if you decide not to charge them up to the bookstall. Otherwise your accounts will not reflect a true picture of the costs involved, and you could also be causing embarrassment to a possible successor. The correct way of doing this is to enter the expenses on the left-hand page, and show the equivalent amount on the Income side as a 'donation'.

Expenses (left-hand page)

		Value	
Date	Invoice No.	£	p
Jan 13	64156	27	00
Feb 2	62327	10	00
10	Cash purchase	1	30
Mar 1	69344	7	25

Sales (right-hand page)

		Value	
Date		£	p
Jan 7		6	25
14		2	40
21		5	80
28		2	35
Feb 4	(Re invoice 64156)	30	00
4		2	05

Annual accounts

At the end of the year you will have to calculate your net profit. This again should present no problems provided you have kept all your records correctly. The following example shows the method of calculation:

	£	£
Total sales		272
Less cost of sales		
Opening stock	54	
Purchases	247	
	301	
Closing stock	58	243
Gross profit		29
Less expenses		7
Net profit		22

It will be seen that both stock control and accounting are really only a matter of being methodical. Trouble only starts when you slip up on the routine work. Get into the habit of making the proper entries at the right time, and you should have no problems. It will only take a few minutes a week.

Check points
* Be methodical.
* Be accurate.
* Be meticulous.
* Write things down. Don't rely on your memory.
* At the end of the year—take stock carefully, and present accurate accounts.

7

The Agent and his Bookseller

One of the most important factors in running a successful bookstall can be your relationship with your supplying bookseller. This short chapter, which incorporates some suggestions from Christian booksellers with a wide experience of Book Agents, offers some advice on what to do, and what not to do, to ensure his friendly co-operation.

Above all, be businesslike. Just because running a bookstall is fun, it does not mean that you should not have a professional approach. You will find it helpful to have some idea of the mechanics of the book trade in general, and bookselling in particular, and the bibliography in Appendix iv includes some useful reading in this respect.

Treat your bookseller with consideration. Remember, you are by no means his only customer. If you have a problem to discuss, don't turn up at his shop without warning, and expect him to give you his full attention. Ring up and make an appointment.

Establish at the very beginning what rules, if any, he has for his Book Agents, and abide by them. They have been devised to make things run smoothly, and not deliberately to thwart you.

For the convenience of both of you, let him know exactly who is authorised to buy books on your account. It has not been unknown for a minister, or another member of the congregation, to buy books for himself on the bookstall account, and forget to mention the fact to the bookstall manager, with resulting embarrassment all round! If you are a registered Book Agent, you will have a number which should be quoted with every order. It is as well not to divulge this number to any except authorised persons. Or you may instruct your bookseller not to supply any orders from your church without your signature.

Some booksellers have a special system for invoicing Book Agents' orders. When you have taken your books to the counter, make it clear that you are an agent *before* the assistant starts counting up your books.

If you have a special request for a large quantity of books, whether for firm sale or on sale or return, place your order well in advance. They may have to be ordered specially from the publisher. Don't expect your bookseller necessarily to have in stock the amount of a particular title that you want for a special meeting that evening.

Be realistic in ordering 'sale or return' books. Don't order more than you think you can reasonably sell. And return any unsold books promptly. Above all, don't over-order on seasonal items. You will not be popular if you order two dozen cut-out Christmas cribs and return 20 unsold on December 27th.

Give at least twenty-four hours' notice if you are phoning through an order to be picked up later.

Don't order single copies of a pamphlet by an obscure publisher. Single copy orders, except from an established publisher with whom he regularly deals, result in a net loss to the bookseller, and you should not expect him to stand this expense. Order any such items direct from the publisher, and expect to pay full price plus postage.

Settle all bills promptly. Christian organisations ought not to run up debts.

Check point
* Treat your bookseller as you would like to be treated yourself.

The final chapters of this book have been contributed by two bookstall managers writing out of their own experience. Jennifer Franklin gives an account of the first few weeks as a bookstall manager in a small town church. Beryl Goodland has been running bookstalls for many years, in both a suburban and a rural area, and has discovered many novel ways of using the church bookstall in outreach to the wider neighbourhood.

8

Birth of a Bookstall

First you need a need . . .
One chilly February evening, as part of a Home
Mission weekend, a coachload of church members
and friends set off to visit the chapel at one of
London's airports. The visit was filled with interest—but for me as a newcomer (my husband had
become minister of the church a few months before)
the highlight had nothing to do with the airport at
all. The chaplain took us into his office for coffee,
and in the room was a revolving bookstand filled
with books. The party converged on this with almost
more enthusiasm than they had showed for the
coffee.

'Here,' I said to myself, 'is a real NEED!'

Start officially
Opportunity to act came six weeks later at our
General Church Meeting. The idea of a bookstall
was suggested, and had vigorous support. But
somebody has to be IN CHARGE (*Bookstall Beginners'*

Rule No. 1). I heard myself offering, and two other voices came at once: 'I'll help.'

So we had our 'responsible person' and a committee of three, which was then given official permission to investigate the possibilities. We were off! 'We' were a minister's wife with a love of books, and access to a whole study-full of religious books, many of which she had never got around to reading; a part-time pharmacist and mother of three teenage boys, who was an avid reader and passed on many books to her friends; and a young man soon to go to college, with a keen evangelistic outlook and an easy manner with people of any age.

Our first impromptu committee meeting happened straight away. We were full of ideas:

'We could have a library of second-hand books as well!' said Barbara.

'What about selling records and cassettes too?' enthused Malcolm.

'Let's start with just books,' I countered faintly, thinking to myself, '*Whatever* have we started?'

Go for the top!

From that moment I realised we must 'be business-like, for God's sake!' (*Bookstall Beginners' Rule No. 2*). This was to be service for the Lord, and only the best would do. But where should we start?

A friend telephoned—would I like to go shopping in a nearby town? I remembered it had two Christian bookshops (our own town has none) and said, 'Yes please!' At both I asked for help. One was friendly but vague. The other was friendly and helpful; I came away with a duplicated handout on running a bookstall, an application form for a Book Agent's licence and—best of all—the telephone number of a lady in my town who was already running a very successful bookstall at her parish church.

In the following days I made numerous telephone calls and had a very helpful session with my bookstall-running neighbour. I was amazed to find myself spending an average of half an hour a day on bookstall matters.

The family were not so much surprised as resigned: 'What's Mum got herself into now?' 'Shall we be able to get books cheap?'

Reporting back

Although clearly one person is needed to be in charge, the back-up committee are vital and must be kept in the picture (*Bookstall Beginners' Rule No. 3*). Barbara and Malcolm got a note each after one week, telling them of my various investigations.

By the end of the second week the picture was becoming clearer: I could talk about Book Agents and retailer's discount and know what I meant! I typed out a statement for my back-up team: 'A church bookstall—what will be required.' Basically this was: a Book Agent's licence; arrangements for supply from two booksellers; helpers to man the stall regularly; a display table with some kind of stands or bookrests; safe storage for these and the books on church premises (this would involve church stewards and property stewards); a date to begin—I suggested the church anniversary, then seven weeks away; and money (a hundred pounds) to buy the first supplies and to meet telephone, stationery and other small expenses.

As I finished it I knew the last item was going to prove the biggest hurdle . . .

Money, money, money . . .
At this time the church's finances were struggling out of the red. Barbara was married to the church treasurer, and she reacted quickly—'*No way* can we ask the church for a hundred pounds!' But she did not lack either faith, or determination. 'We'll have to put off the start for a bit—perhaps make it September?—and do some fund-raising ourselves in the meantime. We certainly mustn't give up, though: this is a venture of faith!'

So I learned that we must not ask the church for money, but ask the Lord. (*Bookstall Beginners' Rule No. 4*—though of course keep in mind that the Lord's advice to *you* may be to ask the church, after all!) That Sunday afternoon I telephoned church stewards and other officers who needed to be kept informed of our progress. Then one of them rang back. 'This is an important idea, I'd like to see it succeed,'—and we had our hundred pounds. I thanked him, of course— but how I thanked the Lord, too!

Now let it start!
The next weeks were full of practical activity, so that I only occasionally had time to think: 'Is this really going to work?'

An interview at the bank established that a

bookstall account would not suffer charges unless it went into the red (little did I realise then how easily that might happen!) and soon a fat paying-in book and a book of large cheques stamped 'Book Agent' made me feel frightfully important. The application for a Book Agent's licence went in, naming the two booksellers we had chosen (one the helpful one that had started me off—was it only three weeks ago?). I wrote to twelve publishers for catalogues, having collected their names and addresses from the title pages of books in one of the shops.

Barbara and Malcolm would help on the first day, and we asked some ladies to provide coffee, too, before the morning service. Then we prepared a 'press release' for the May church newsletter—no going back now! (*Bookstall Beginners' Rule No. 5*: publicise!)

We fixed a date for the committee to meet, mainly to sift catalogues and choose the books for our very first order. In the meantime, we faced the not-too-easy question of just where and how the bookstall itself would be set up.

Your small corner
The bookstall lady at the parish church had a permanent corner where the books stayed, for the large Sunday congregations and for the visitors who came to see the beautiful building during the week. Our set-up was quite different: a small fairly modern nonconformist building on a council estate, with a morning congregation of forty to fifty; an L-shaped vestibule with doors in every wall; and rather than

being available to visitors, the books would have to be protected, even during the hour of service, from the local 'visitors' who caused the disappearance of items from time to time.

In addition, we discovered we had a property steward with grave doubts about the whole venture.

'May we use this table, in the corner of the vestibule, and move it into the hall during the service? We have checked, and the Sunday School is not needing it at present.'

'No problem,' he told us. 'If the Sunday School needs it, they'll probably find the bookstall has folded up by then anyway.'

In the face of this pessimism we went out and spent four pounds on material for a plain dark brown tablecloth. But books really do need a vertical display (*Bookstall Beginners' Rule No. 6*). What could we do about that?

Other people's cast-offs

The only brochure I had of bookstall furniture looked very expensive. Were there other manufacturers? All religious bookshops were well stocked with display stands; they must know, I reasoned, so I rang a couple.

'I think,' said one lady, 'that you have come to the right place. We are moving shop in June, and have far more than we need . . .' On my next visit to her shop, she took me behind the scenes, and I came away with three 'booksteps' for table display, and a promise of something larger nearer the date of their move. And all free!

The booksteps needed some attention, and Malcolm came into his own. At home, I earmarked an even larger corner of the store room for bookstall 'clobber'.

The committee commits itself

The committee met, with more than a fortnight to go before the big day. We discussed small but important details—a cash box, a method of recording sales, and a record file that must be kept of all books. (*Bookstall Beginners' Rule No. 7*: small details matter).

Tables with booksteps on had been tried out at the church; two shelves of a lockable cupboard in the vestry were available for storage. We agreed that both bookselling and coffee must cease abruptly five minutes before service time; we were aiming to complement the worship, not compete with it.

Then, with muted shouts of enthusiasm, we tackled the pile of catalogues—what fun it was! What (or should it be Who?) guided our choice? To many it would have seemed haphazard. We chose all paperbacks, apart from a selection of Bibles in a modern translation. We chose new titles, and some old favourites. We tried to mix easy-reading biographies with straighter stuff; charismatic material with classics like *The Imitation of Christ*. By special request we chose a wide selection of prayer books and books on prayer. We added a few children's books. Some titles were included with a query; it is hard to judge from a catalogue, better to check when in the shop.

We ended the evening with a much-corrected list

of some three dozen titles, knowing we should find others in the shop when we collected these. We fixed a collection day and felt satisfied we had done all we could.

Booked!

Collecting the books was exciting; trying to choose extra ones was frustrating. We were suddenly apprehensive. Then, there they were—a small carton (how few £64-worth looked!) on the back seat of the car. The boot was overloaded with a splendid metal book trolley from the shop-on-the-move, as promised.

Every book was entered on a file card, invoices checked, some publicity posters chosen for the church notice-board, and a list of titles typed which were to be crossed off as books were sold. Later, we found this method cumbersome, and now we write the titles of books sold on a pad, instead.

I had asked the visiting preacher to let me have three minutes of the service in which to talk about the bookstall (*Bookstall Beginners' Rule No. 8*: book talks do work!). What I needed to say took more like three hours to prepare, of course. And we prayed that God would bless this new opportunity.

So our bookstall began.

Reflections and reactions

Since that first Sunday the bookstall has been available for two half-hour periods, before and after morning service, and for special occasions such as our two-day Flower Festival. Turnover topped a hundred pounds after eight weeks, but we expect some Sundays to sell none at all. Many books have been ordered for individuals, especially Bibles and hymnbooks, and regular supplies of Bible reading booklets. Best of all, the bookstall has become a familiar focal point on Sunday morning. We have tried to have new titles, or a poster, or even just a new punchline (e.g. 'These books cost less than a gallon of petrol') every week.

The books look very few! The ones we think will sell well don't—we still have much to learn; but sometimes the book we are doubtful about does sell, or someone who has said they 'don't read' comes and buys one. People come back to enthuse to us about what they have bought; then our spirits lift!

Many of us recognise that at our church we need our spiritual horizons widened, and a bookstall can help, because through it we can be in real contact with authors whom we may never meet. It is a continuing responsibility, and we have bad moments wondering if we will be left with books on our hands; but it is such a positive activity, with such limitless scope, that it is always exciting.

We hope others who read this will find this is true for them, too.

Footnote: When I hastened to tell our generous donor that our turnover had reached a hundred pounds, he said, 'Then if you do no more than this, it will have been worth while.'

Jennifer R. Franklin

9

Outreach in the Community

'Spreading the Word about Books' was the headline in a local newspaper over a story about a book event we had organised in a nearby market town. The words sum up my philosophy on bookselling. It is so important to spread out from our static church bookstalls, to reach people who never enter a church building—or for that matter a Christian bookshop.

There are many ways in which Christian literature can be brought to the people, ranging from small neighbourhood events to highly organised book fairs.

To take the simplest first—

Book parties
A good Book Agent is always glad to encourage others to find potential new customers. So I was delighted when one of my friends volunteered to hold a book party in her home.

We fixed a suitable date and time, and she sent out invitations to her neighbours. Several hours before the event her home was transformed into a bookshop. (Always allow plenty of time to get ready; there is nothing worse than trying to set books out as people are arriving!)

To get the party going, guests took part in a game which involved matching up authors and titles. There followed a brief introductory talk describing the various types of books available, and the age-groups for which they were intended. Children's books were well to the fore.

Soon the guests were happily browsing and chatting, while small piles of purchased books grew steadily larger.

Book parties can be repeated time and again in any locality. They can be held at any time of day, and are especially successful in the pre-Christmas season. Several features can be incorporated, such as book reviews, prepared in advance by some of those present; a film strip; a short talk by an author, etc.—not forgetting a cup of coffee!

Literary lunches
Most housewives enjoy eating a meal which they have not had to prepare. When we advertised our first Ladies' Literary Luncheon, we sold nearly a hundred invitation cards, which had been attractively designed and printed by a local printer.

We used our church premises, which had good facilities for serving a three-course meal; but you could equally well use a restaurant, by arrangement with the manager.

The guest speaker was a sales representative for

a group of Christian publishers, and we also featured an interview with a well-known writer of children's books, who lives locally. Afterwards, guests were able to browse around the books on display—and buy!

The luncheon was such a success that on future occasions we had to drop the word 'Ladies', as husbands and men friends asked to be allowed to come.

Book fairs

The literary luncheon just described was one event in a week-long book fair, through which we set out to involve all sections of the local community.

It can be difficult to get people to visit a book fair held on church premises, especially when the church, like ours, was situated at some distance from the main shopping centre. We decided to lay on some added attractions.

Read-in

The fair was launched with a day-long 'read-in' of the whole of the New Testament in a modern translation. Previous to the event, a chart was displayed in the foyer of the church, divided into quarter-hour sections, and people were invited to enter their names for the times which they felt able to allocate to reading aloud. Reading started with Matthew 1 at 7 a.m., and the last chapter of Revelation ended at 1.45 the following morning. Throughout the day, people dropped into the church to listen, and the reading was also relayed into the church hall, where books were displayed for sale.

A spotlight highlights

It takes a lot of books to make a proper show in the average church hall. We needed to find some way of filling the corners.

The local Floral Art Society was asked to help organise a competition. Competitors were given a preview of a number of books, from which they had to select one to illustrate the title with a flower arrangement. The result was a very colourful display, with each floral arrangement standing beside a copy of the chosen book.

Local talent

Another part of the hall was used for displaying (not selling) books by local authors, whose interests ranged from motor racing to theology. A letter in the local newspaper elicited a response from several writers who lived in the area, and also a letter from the Deputy Borough Librarian, offering the services of the Reference Library.

We discovered that, in addition to the thirty-two living authors represented (eleven of whom were known to be Christians), our borough had at various times in the past housed such eminent literary figures as Matthew Arnold, Charles Kingsley, Mary Shelley and Richard Brinsley Sheridan—not to mention Mrs Beeton of cookery book fame.

Involving the children

A children's art and handwriting competition attracted parents who came to see their offsprings' work displayed. The children had been asked to design a cover for a book soon to be published by the Scripture Union, entitled *Rich Man, Poor Man* – one child showed the rich man as a car owner, while the poor man was pumping up his bicycle tyre! Those who were not so good at drawing were invited to write out the twenty-third psalm inside a decorated border.

Bible exhibition

Yet another corner of the hall held a display of Bibles in many languages, loaned by the Bible Society. A lady from Japan asked to be allowed to borrow a Bible in Japanese, and as a result was presented with the copy by the society. A similar exhibition could be tried in a multi-racial area.

Books in the classroom

In order to reach our local school, we sent a carton of selected children's books to the headmistress for her to look at. She was so impressed with the quality that she sent the box round to each member of the staff, and told them to order what they wanted.

Schools often have special funds which they can allocate for a purpose such as this, or after seeing the books they may prefer to obtain them through their normal channels.

Making it known

Advertising of book fairs and similar events is most

important. There are other ways of doing this besides the liberal use of posters and hand-outs.

The year the Bible Society published *Good News for Modern Man*, we obtained a number of their display stands, each holding three books, to which we attached a sticker giving details of our book fair. We then approached a number of shopkeepers, and ended up by having free publicity in thirty-five shop windows. 'Good News' was seen among the newspapers, beside loaves of bread, next to the apples and oranges, on plush carpets, alongside spinning laundry, and on the fish slab.

Each bookstand held a copy of the Good News New Testament, and two other books which we tried to match to the shop concerned. A wedding photographer displayed *I Married You*, and a book of photographs of the Holy Land, as well as a photograph of a minister handing a Bible to a newly-married couple in wheelchairs.

This type of advertising was time-consuming, as each shop was personally visited three times—in the first instance to show a sample and gain permission, then to deliver the stand, and finally to remove it. On the last visit, each shop manager was given the copy of the New Testament. This gift was financed by church members who earmarked their envelopes 'Good News for modern shopkeepers'. Many of the shopkeepers asked to buy the other books which had been displayed. We like to think they had been having a quiet read.

Building societies will often allow their windows to be used for display purposes. As our local manager said, 'An attractive display will encourage people to look into the window more than a percentage notice!' A window must be booked several months in advance.

It can be a daunting prospect to be faced with a space measuring fifteen feet by three, which must be filled. An advertising agent told me it is a recognised fact that one has two and a half seconds in which to catch the eye of the passer-by, 'so be bold, be clear and be uncluttered.'

The first time we used a window was during a Christian Book Week. The posters that year featured a large bubble bearing details of the Book Week, and this bubble we cut out of several posters, using a sharp scalpel rather than scissors, to ensure a clean edge. The posters were then backed with bright green card, on to which two books were mounted. To do this, slits were cut in the card, and transparent perspex book rests were inserted.

The 'bubbles' were stuck directly on to the window, using Scotch Spray Mount, which enables the poster to be peeled off cleanly when it is no longer needed. Any slight mark cleans off easily with lighter fuel.

The corners of the window were filled with cardboard rolls of all sizes, from the inside of toilet rolls to carpet rolls, all covered with brightly coloured gift-wrap paper, and topped with cardboard cones to form giant pencils.

Go to the top
I stood one morning in our local department store,

watching the endless stream of shoppers criss-crossing its way through the building. What an opportunity for book sales, I thought.

Easter was fast approaching so, armed with a suitable Easter book for children, I paid a personal visit to the manager's office. (Nothing succeeds like a personal encounter—letters often land in the waste paper basket.)

I suggested that, since this was a Christian festival, it would be good to see an Easter selection of books on display. On hearing that my husband was the minister of a church, he told me, 'Like your husband, I also have to consult higher authority!' In due time, however, permission was given for a bookstall to be set up in the store for a week. I was to be personally responsible for staffing it, and keeping it well stocked with books. The money taken was also kept separate from the general store monies.

The manager took me on a conducted tour in order to find the best location and eventually suggested the entrance to the restaurant area on the second floor. He even sent his display manager to assist in setting out the book area, decorating it with several mobiles and objects connected with Easter which had been made by school children. Bibles and books for all ages which were connected with the Easter theme were on display.

This was an occasion when the witness was as important as the selling. The store made no charge for our use of their space, though we did give them a small monetary donation.

Think big

The International Year of the Child gave us the opportunity for our biggest venture yet. We approached the local council for permission to hold a children's book fair in the market place of Ross-on-Wye, a country town which is also a tourist centre. The site was an ideal one, as the market place is in front of the library, right in the centre of the town. (Always apply for the best possible site at the earliest possible date—the authorities can only refuse!)

We chose two days during the school holidays, ensuring that neither day was early closing. (An eye to detail in planning can save a lot of wasted effort and disappointment on the part of volunteer helpers.)

We needed a good variety of books to make an impact on such a large site. Two-thirds of these were supplied by the Christian bookshops with whom I am registered as a Book Agent. Four other local bookshops readily responded by supplying a quantity of good children's classics, and also making frequent visits to the market during the day to replenish the stock. I did not ask them for a financial contribution, but they voluntarily gave us a ten per cent discount on all sales.

The library also co-operated by displaying information about their services for children.

Borrowed trestle tables were covered with cloth, and colourful wall friezes made borders for the tables. The collection of bookstands I had acquired over the years were put to good use. We made display panels from light-weight ceiling board off-cuts. Bright pink lettering on a black background read 'The International Year of the Child—Every Child has the Right to Grow with Good Books.' Bold animal posters were supplied by the publishers of the books featured in the special issue postage stamps commemorating the Year of the Child. These adorned the pillars of the market-place. We also made our own posters—of which the most eye-catching was a three-foot disc with a sky-blue background, showing an owl encircled by fluorescent orange cut-out letters reading, 'LOOK—BOOKS'. You don't have to spend a lot of money to make an effective show.

The market place project proved to be very exciting and very worthwhile. We sold continuously throughout the two days, apart from a short lull during the lunch hour. It showed conclusively the importance of going where the people are. A few weeks previously we had organised a similar outreach in a church hall in Gloucester, but on that occasion we had long periods of inactivity as we hopefully waited for customers.

Say it with words
From a large-scale project, back to something in which we can all play a part.

As a nurse, I have viewed with pleasure and dismay the bouquets which arrive at the beds of patients from those who 'say it with flowers'. Why not encourage relatives and friends to 'say it with WORDS'? They last longer!

One hospital authority allowed a rack of books to be sold at the hospital shop for a short period. This is an outlet for Christian books which is well worth investigating further. Another is through hospital radio, in the form of book reviews or the reading of selected passages; or even a serialised story for a hospital caring for long-stay patients. The possibilities are endless—if not for actually selling books, at least for spreading the word.

It's the message that matters

The advertisement on television is trying first to sell you toothpaste—not a dazzling smile. We on the other hand are not trying first to sell a book, but the *message* of the book. It is our job as Book Agents to catch the attention of a person so that his interest in a book is aroused—then to make him want to read it, and then, if possible, to sell him a copy.

'These things have been written that you may believe . . . and have life' (John 20.30).

We may never know how far-reaching our efforts may be.

My brother, who was a missionary surgeon in Thailand, was visiting our church when in England on leave. Instead of a preaching fee, he asked for a selection of books to be sent to his Thai medical students. Among these was David Adeney's *Chinese Christians Face the Revolution*, and he suggested to them that this book should be translated into Thai.

Some time later, there was a coup in Thailand and a right wing military government came into power. All suspected communistic literature was burned—including this red-covered book. However, a government official stuffed a copy into his pocket. On reading it later, he discovered his mistake—and was so impressed that the government had copies printed and given free of charge to all the students in Bangkok.

Perhaps, if we had not had a bookstall open in church that Sunday night, all that might never have happened.

Beryl Goodland

APPENDICES

THE PUBLISHERS ASSOCIATION

19 BEDFORD SQUARE, LONDON WC1B 3HJ

APPLICATION FOR A BOOK AGENT'S LICENCE

A registration fee of Five Pounds, seventy five pence (inc. VAT) should be enclosed with this application.

Name of applicant ....
(If you have a business organizational or institutional name please show it).

Address of applicant ....

....

1 The applicant nominates for the said licence the following bookseller(s) whose willingness to supply has been ascertained:
   (Please give full names and addresses)

....

....

2 What type of books do you propose to sell?

....

3 How much stock of books do you propose to carry?
   (Indicate number of volumes and value)

....

4 Describe the manner in which you propose to sell these books

....

....

....

5 How do you propose to display the books to intending customers?

....

....

6 What special connections have you, if any, to facilitate the sale of books?

....

....

....

Date   (Signature)
VAT Reg. No. 233 577 359   P.T.O.

APPENDIX I

Book Agents Licences are granted in consideration of an undertaking by the Licensee

(i) not to offer for sale or to sell any new net book or books at less than the full net published price, either directly or indirectly or by way of settlement discount;

(ii) not to ask for or to accept any allowance upon new net books except from the Bookseller named upon this Licence or upon any endorsement thereof.

No.

THE PUBLISHERS ASSOCIATION

19 BEDFORD SQUARE, LONDON, WC1B 3HJ

BOOK AGENT'S LICENCE

Name
(If you have a business name, please show it)

Address

having applied for recognition as a Book Agent, and having given the undertaking printed on the back of this Licence, is hereby authorised to purchase new books: for resale to the public at the full published price, from the following bookseller, viz.,

RELIGIOUS BOOKS ONLY

and the said bookseller is hereby authorised to allow the said book agent an allowance not exceeding fifty per centum of the retail discount given to the bookseller by the publisher in respect of each new book supplied to the book agent, BUT ONLY during the period for which this Licence is valid, and so long as the Licensee observes the conditions of his undertaking.

It is a condition of the granting of this Licence that it may be revoked at any time by the Publishers Association upon reason being given and upon its giving written notice by the hand of its Secretary to the parties named herein. But unless revoked on account of any action which the Publishers Association or the Joint Advisory Committee consider to be a breach of its terms and/or conditions three months' notice shall be given to the Licensee.

For and on behalf of
the Publishers Association

....*Secretary*

Date of Issue

[P.T.O.

UNDERTAKING

This Licence is granted in consideration of an undertaking by the Licensee:

(i) not to offer for sale or to sell any new net book or books at less than the full net published price, either directly or indirectly or by way of settlement discount;

(ii) not to ask for or to accept any allowance upon new net books except from the Bookseller named upon this Licence or upon any endorsement thereof.

I/WE accept the terms and conditions of this Licence and undertake that they shall be observed in all dealings under its authority.

Signature of Licensee...
(in full)

Business name (if any)...

Business address..

....

....

Date..

APPENDIX III

USEFUL ADDRESSES

General

Booksellers' Association of Great Britain and Ireland, 154 Buckingham Palace Road, London SW1W 9TZ. Publishes annually a list of members and also of religious bookshops who are members. Has a Religious Booksellers' sub-group.

Publishers Association, 19 Bedford Square, London WC1B 3HJ. Publishes list of members. Has a Religious Publishers' sub-group.

Independent Publishers Guild, 120 Pentonville Road, London N1 9JN.

Irish Publishers Association, 8 Herbert Place, Dublin 2.

National Book League, 7 Albemarle Street, London W1X 4BB.

Christian

Christian Bookstall Managers' Association, Hon. Sec. 595 Walsall Road, Great Wyrley, Walsall, WS6 6AE.

Feed the Minds—Joint Action for Christian Literature Overseas, Supports Christian literature projects worldwide. SPCK, 4DU; or USCL, Luke House, Farnham Road, Guildford, Surrey, GU1 4XD.

Fellowship of Christian Writers, Hon. Sec., 30 The Vale, Southgate, London N14 6HP.

Torch Trust for the Blind, Torch House, Hallaton, Market Harborough, Leics., LE16 8UJ. Provides Christian literature on cassette and in large type, Braille and Moon. For sale and lending library. Also various magazines, for adults and children.

APPENDIX IV

USEFUL PUBLICATIONS

On church bookstalls
Christian Literature and the Church Bookstall, Timothy Dudley-Smith (Falcon, 1963) now out of print.
Church Bookstalls, David Rudiger (Falcon, 1971). Booklet.
A Handbook for Christian Bookstall Managers (Christian Bookstall Managers Association)

Reference books
British Books in Print (J. Whitaker & Sons Ltd., annually)
Cumulative Book List (quarterly, as above)
Paperbacks in Print (annually, as above)
Religion and Theology (SCM Press, annually)
Religious Books in Print, 1974 (Whitaker). Published only in one year, but still useful if you can find a copy.
Writers' and Artists' Yearbook (A. & C. Black, annually). Along with much other information relevant to books and writing, gives the names and addresses of the major publishers in Great Britain and Ireland, Commonwealth and USA, and names the type of publishing in which each specialises.

General background to the book trade
Beginning in Bookselling, Irene Babbidge (Andre Deutsch, revised edn. 1972)
The Bookselling Business, Thomas Joy (Pitman, 1974)
Opening a bookshop. Some of your questions answered (Booksellers Association)
Selling the Book. A bookshop promotion manual, ed. Sydney Hyde (Clive Bingley, 1977)

The Truth about Publishing, Stanley Unwin (Allen & Unwin, revised edn. 1976)

Some newspapers and journals carrying reviews of Christian books
Weekly

Baptist Times, 4 Southampton Row, London WC1 B 4AB

British Weekly, Bible House, 146 Queen Victoria Street, London EC4V 4EH (non-denominational)

Catholic Herald, Lambs Passage, Bunhill Row, London EC1Y 8TQ

Christian Herald, 26 Grafton Road, Worthing, Sussex, BN11 1QU (non-denominational)

Christian Record, Bible House, 146 Queen Victoria Street, London EC4V 4EH (non-denominational)

Church of England Newspaper, Bible House, 146 Queen Victoria Street, London EC4V 4EH

Church of Ireland Gazette, 48 Bachelor's Walk, Lisburn, Co. Antrim

Church Times, 7 Portugal Street, London WC2A 2HP (Anglican)

Elim Evangel, P.O. Box 38, Cheltenham, Glos.

English Churchman, P.O. Box 27, London SE5 8NP (Evangelical Anglican) Fortnightly

East-West Digest, 139 Petersham Road, Petersham, Richmond, Surrey, TW10 7AA (Eastern Orthodox interest). Fortnightly

Methodist Recorder, 176 Fleet Street, London EC4A 2EP

Scottish Catholic Observer, Catholic Herald Ltd., 19 Waterloo Street, Glasgow C2

The Universe, 21 Fleet Street, London EC4Y 1AP (Catholic)

The War Cry, The Salvation Army, 101 Queen Victoria Street, London EC4I 4EP

Monthly

Buzz, 51 Haydons Road, London SW19 1HG

Challenge, the Good News Paper, Challenge Literature Fellowship, Revenue Buildings, Chapel Road, Worthing, West Sussex, BN11 1BQ (non-denominational tabloid)

Clergy Review, Heythrop College, Cavendish Square, London W1M OAN (Catholic)

Crusade, 19 Draycott Place, London SW3 2SJ (non-denominational)

Churchman's Magazine, Protestant Truth Society, 184 Fleet Street, London EC4 (bi-monthly)

Evangelism Today, 320 Ashley Down Road, Bristol

Evangelical Times, 14 Silverleigh Road, Thornton Heath, Surrey, CR4 6DU (non-denominational)

Floodtide, Christian Literature Crusade, 203 Church Road, London SE19

Life and Work, 121 George Street, Edinburgh, EH2 4YN (Church of Scotland)

Family, 51 Haydons Road, London SW19 1HG

The Month, 114 Mount Street, London W1 (Catholic)

New Blackfriars, Blackfriars, Oxford (Catholic)

The Officer, The Salvation Army, 101 Queen Victoria Street, London EC4I 4EP

Redemption Tidings, 106–114 Talbot Street, Nottingham NG1 5GH (Assemblies of God)

Reform, 8 Tavistock Place, London WC1H 9RT (United Reformed Church)

Scottish Baptist Magazine, Baptist Union of Scotland, 14 Aytoun Road, Glasgow, G41 5RT

The Tablet, 48 Great Peter Street, London SW1P 2HB (Catholic)

Theology, SPCK, Holy Trinity Church, Marylebone Road, London NW1 4DU

Third Way, 19 Draycott Place, London SW3 2SJ (non-denominational)

Welsh Churchman, Woodland Place, Penarth, Glam., CF6 2EX

Quarterly

Baptist Quarterly, 4 Southampton Row, London WC1B 4AB

A Bookstalls Newsletter, A. Guy Taylor, 11 Thorpe Chase, Ripon, North Yorks, HG4 1UA

Catholic Truth, Catholic Truth Society, 38–40 Eccleston Square, London SW1V 1PD (twice yearly)

Christian Graduate, Universities and Colleges Christian Fellowship, 38 de Montfort Street, Leicester, LE1 7GP

The Churchman, 7 Wine Office Court, Fleet Street, London EC4A 3DA (Evangelical Anglican)

Evangelical Quarterly, The Paternoster Press, 3 Mount Radford Crescent, Exeter EX2 4JW

Heythrop Journal, 114 Mount Street, London W1 (Catholic)

CRY HOSANNA

Betty Pulkingham and Mimi Farra (Ed.)

Sequel to *Sound of Living Waters* and *Fresh Sounds*

CRY HOSANNA is a collection of more than 140 songs and hymns which represent God's praising people around the world. It contains many strong hymns from varied traditions. As in the case of its predecessors, the songs have been selected because of their proven usefulness in worship, teaching and celebration. Most appear together for the first time.

'All over the world Christians are discovering new freedom in praise as they draw together to worship the living God,' say the editors. 'Most of us have been bound at some point to the particular tradition out of which we come, and have needed the Spirit's driving wind to dislodge us from the place where we were "stuck". The same Spirit who drove Jesus into the wilderness will drive us into similar places of exposure, challenge and blessing. It is there that we will learn to cry "Hosanna".'

Most songs appear with guitar chords as well as simple piano accompaniment. The volume is spiral-bound for easy usage. Ideal for church and family worship.

CHASING THE DRAGON

Jackie Pullinger

Love took her
to the darkness
of the Walled City

One of the most dramatic Christian autobiographies ever published – 'The Cross and Switchblade' for the 1980s.

Inside the British Crown Colony of Hong Kong squats the Walled City. Strangers are unwelcome. Police hesitate to enter. It is a haven for drug smuggling and illegal gambling. Prostitution, pornography and heroin addiction flourish. Thirty thousand people – maybe twice that – live in a few cramped acres.

When Jackie Pullinger set out from England she had no idea that God was calling her to the Walled City. Yet as she spoke of Jesus Christ, brutal Triad gangsters were converted, prostitutes quit, and Jackie discovered a new treatment for drug addiction: the baptism of the Holy Spirit.

A tough, honest account of one girl's dedication and courage.

THE HOLY BIBLE
NEW INTERNATIONAL VERSION

The *New International Version* has been enthusiastically welcomed by Christians everywhere. Nearly **three million** have been sold world-wide. This entirely fresh translation by an international team of more than one hundred scholars, the fruit of fifteen years' labour, has been described by Dr Billy Graham as 'one of the most thorough attempts yet made to convey original meaning. It preserves, in a sense, a certain historic familiarity, but couches God's message in contemporary and easily understood terms.'

A copy of the NIV should be at every Christian's side. 'We are convinced that it is by far the best translation in English,' says Dr Francis Schaeffer. Lorne C. Sanny, President of the Navigators, describes the NIV as 'my constant companion since publication'. The *New York Times* called it 'a major publishing phenomenon'. 'What bowls you over as you read the New International Version,' commented Peter Grosvenor in the *Daily Express*, 'is quite how much of the old Bible you misunderstood.'

The *New International Version Bible* is available in a wide variety of editions, including standard and popular editions, leather bindings, paperbacks and pocket editions. It is a must for every bookstall.